Contradiction and Conflict

*The 1988
Education Act
in Action*

David Coulby
and
Leslie Bash

CASSELL

Cassell Educational Limited
Villiers House
41/47 Strand
London WC2N 5JE
England

387 Park Avenue South
New York, NY 10016–8810

First published 1991

British Library Cataloguing in Publication Data
Contradiction and conflict: the 1988 Education Act in
    action.
    1. England. Education. Law
    I. Coulby, David   II. Bash, Leslie
    344.2047

ISBN   0-304-32391-8 (hardback)
          0-304-32390-X (paperback)

Typeset by Colset Pte Ltd, Singapore
Printed and bound in Great Britain by
Biddles Ltd, Guildford and King's Lynn

*This book is
dedicated to
Jonathan Coulby
and David Bash*

Contents

Acknowledgements

The three years we have spent observing the formulation, adoption and implementation of the 1988 Education Act have inevitably placed a strain on the other members of both our families. Our first acknowledgement is to them for their persistent support and patience. Early drafts of Chapters 1, 2, 3 and 8 were seen by Christine Eden, Valerie Richards and Stephen Ward. Our thanks to them: their comments led to significant changes but the errors remain our own. Part of Chapter 4 draws upon work carried out with Tony Edwards and Sharon Gewirtz on an ESRC-funded research project (C00232462) on city technology colleges. The authors of Chapter 4 are also specifically grateful to David Halpin, John Fitz, Rosalind Levacic, Brian Knight, Stephen Ball, Anne Gold and Richard Bowe for permission to draw upon unpublished papers on the effects of the Reform Act.

Abbreviations

AT	Attainment Target
BTEC	Business and Technician Education Council
CPVE	Certificate of Pre-vocational Education
CRE	Commission for Racial Equality
CTC	city technology college
EATE	Enterprise Awareness in Teacher Education
EHE	Enterprise in Higher Education
EPA	educational priority area
GMS	grant-maintained school
HSU	History Study Unit
ILEA	Inner London Education Authority
INSET	in-service education of teachers
LEA	local education authority
LEATGS	Local Education Authority Training Grant Scheme
LMS	local management of schools
MSC	Manpower Services Commission
NAB	National Advisory Body for Higher Education
NAHT	National Association of Head Teachers
NATFHE	National Association of Teachers in Further and Higher Education
NCC	National Curriculum Council
NCVQ	National Council for Vocational Qualifications
PALs	Planned Admission Levels
PC	Profile Component
PCFC	Polytechnic and Colleges Funding Council

Abbreviations

PGCE	Post Graduate Certificate of Education
SACRE	Standing Advisory Councils on Religious Education
SAT	Standard Assessment Task
SEAC	School Examinations and Assessment Council
TA	Teacher Assessment
TECs	Training and Enterprise Councils
TGAT	Task Group on Assessment and Testing
TVEI	Technical and Vocational Education Initiative
UFC	Universities Funding Council
WG	Working Group
YOP	Youth Opportunities Programme
YTS	Youth Training Scheme

1

Introduction: The 1988 Education Act and Themes of Government Policy

David Coulby

THE IMPORTANCE OF THE ACT

The 1988 Education Reform Act is a major component of government policy. Along with the legislation on the community charge (poll tax), it is the most important achievement of the third Thatcher government. The ideas and policies behind it were among the main planks of the political platform on which the Conservative Party fought and won the 1987 general election. It brings about the most far-reaching changes to the education system of England and Wales since the 1944 Education Act. Because of the magnitude of these changes which it is bringing about, it probably represents the most important positive government intervention in any area of social policy since Margaret Thatcher became Prime Minister in 1979.

An earlier book (Bash and Coulby, 1989) described the social, economic and political forces which led to the formulation and adoption of the Act. It outlined the Act's major intentions and indicated how these were likely to work out in practice. Since that book contented itself with the likely outcomes of policy implementation rather than venturing into wider social prediction, its forecasts have, to a very large extent, been validated. The pattern of implementation over the past two years has, nevertheless, thrown up difficulties, opposition, support and resolutions which go beyond what could have been foreseen two years ago. The present book updates progress on the implementation of the 1988 Act for the benefit of the reader who does not have ready access to the deluge of paper from the Department of Education and Science (DES), the National Curriculum Council (NCC), the School Examinations and Assessment Council (SEAC), the local education authorities (LEAs) and many others, which has been the accompaniment to and, to a certain extent, the mode of its implementation. The book is intended to address two types of readership: those concerned with the detail of current government policy on education in England and Wales and those concerned with the politics of the implementation of large-scale social policy.

The themes of conflict and contradiction need not be seen as specific to the 1988 Act. Any social policy initiative of this extent and magnitude is likely to generate conflict, not least from those who see themselves as the losers from any resulting changes. Similarly, social policy legislation will have its unintended as well as its intended outcomes and will fit with varying degrees of symmetry alongside other government policies, especially those on finance. It is, nevertheless, the contention of this book that the Act contains a particularly high level of contradiction both within itself and with other areas of the policy of the government which introduced it. These contradictions are in some cases a matter of political philosophy or ideology as, say, between the urge to decentralize school budgets via formula funding and the local management of schools (LMS) whilst simultaneously centralizing the whole curriculum for children between the ages of 5 and 16. In other cases the contradictions are actually at the level of economic policy as, say, the contradiction between the urge to save money by encouraging the rationalization of secondary schooling within LEAs and the policy which allows schools to opt out of LEA control, thereby effectively eliminating the LEA's power to proceed with rationalization.

Some of the conflict generated by the Act is as a result of these contradictions but other conflicts are a matter of political or educational opposition to the Act in terms either of the detail of its implementation or of its more general intentions and philosophy. The following chapters tend to treat contradictions and conflict as if they were invariably connected. Whilst this might not always be the case – indeed protagonists might heighten or even invent contradictions in order to engage in a conflict which is actually macro-political – the advantage of exploring the sites of conflict is that it allows examination of those areas where contradiction is at its most visible.

The link between contradiction and conflict may be taken further than this. Contradiction, as used in the following chapters, implies the ways in which one aspect of policy tends to negate another. However, the term also implies a further meaning: that of conflict, and in particular class conflict. The policy contradictions identified here are in fact often related to wider aspects of class conflict and the way in which state policy attempts to participate in such conflict. Similarly, the political philosophies and ideologies mentioned above are likely to relate to a system of ideas and beliefs predicated upon the class position of those who uphold and propagate them. The ideologies used to legitimate the Act and those which it seeks to propagate are ultimately related to the class interests of its exponents. The contradictions within the Act, then, can be related to wider conflicts of production and reproduction. At this level at least there is an inescapable connection between contradiction and conflict. The treatment here is to look mainly at the self-negating aspects of contradiction within the Act, but the wider implications are a matter of regular reference. Indeed a major underlying question which all the following chapters seek centrally to address is: to what extent has the adoption and implementation of the policies of the 1988 Act served to improve the education of children and young people from families which do not have access to substantial wealth?

The Act is not addressed to the fee-paying schools. They are, for instance, explicitly excluded from the National Curriculum and testing which are to be compulsory in state schools. For the people who formulated and adopted it, the Act, with the exception of its higher education chapter, is legislation for other people's children. If it is to fulfil the claims made for it in terms of 'raising standards', then it is the state school children who must be so benefited. It is those children from families without ready access to wealth or power who need improvements in education to give them enhanced access, say, to higher education. To interrogate the Act as to the assistance it offers to such children is then reasonable within the terms of the aims of its formulators. This interrogation inevitably explores the possibility of contradiction and class conflict between legislators with explicit middle-class interests and potential beneficiaries of the legislation who are predominantly working class.

The following chapters deal with all the major aspects of the Act in all the phases of the education system. Not surprisingly, the Act remains the major focus of government education policy and no further legislation in this area of social policy has so far been announced. The extent to which the original intentions of the architect of the Act have been modified in practice is dealt with in the individual chapters. Although there have been significant alterations, the main plans of the Act remain intact. Furthermore, they are being implemented with a speed and rigour which have not always characterized educational policy in England and Wales. The successful and rapid implementation of this legislation remains a major priority of government activity. The final chapter places this activity in the context of other government policies and initiatives. However, in order better to contextualize the intervening chapters some introduction to the wider policy issues is provided here. The important strands of government policy of which the Act forms a significant if uneasy part may, at this stage, be summarized under four headings; popularism, privatization, financial control, and centralization. The rest of this chapter examines each of these in turn, with references forward to the other chapters, in order to contextualize their contents within the framework of wider government policy and provide a thematic introduction to the contents of the rest of the book.

Popularism

Margaret Thatcher's three election successes cannot be explained away as the result of fractures within the political opposition. The policies formulated and adopted by her governments have had considerable popular appeal to people without the wealth and power normally associated with Conservative Party supporters. Among the popular themes which her governments have been able to adopt are notions of nationhood, national role, destiny, heritage and tradition. Within this theme the aspirations of democracy and free-enterprise capitalism have successfully been conflated. Another popularist strand has been the critique and debunking of the self-interest and incompetence of professionals and experts. This critique has been highly selective: it has been applied to teachers, social workers, broadcasters, academics, opticians, ambulance workers and medical doctors, but not to the police, the armed forces or business-people. Indeed this latter group have been seen to carry almost a sacred wisdom and their control over the administration of wide areas of social policy has been encouraged. The 1988 Act itself is an important component of the appeal to popularism and consolidates many of these themes: the traditionalist National Curriculum, lots of tests and assemblies, and attacks on familiar folk-devils such as LEAs, teachers and academics all form part of its attempt to appeal beyond the educational establishment to a broader popular constituency. The power of business-people over other professional groups has become consolidated in the new boards of governors of further education (FE) colleges, polytechnics, higher education colleges and, to a lesser extent, schools. The success of the three Thatcher administrations was derived in no small part from the ability to sense popular feeling and to use this as a basis for policy. This can be seen on the one hand in the sale of council houses or Girobank and on the other in the heightening of controls on trade unions or football supporters. This popularism works in at least two ways: as well as itself providing an apparently inexhaustible supply of electoral support, it also serves to fracture the cohesiveness of any opposition. As each person struggles to find wealth and status in the property-owning, share-owning democracy, any sense of group cohesiveness has been undermined. Groups and individuals are increasingly fractured in their opposition to others, be they black people, trade unionists, youth, the loony left or the educational establishment.

The now discredited poll tax is not necessarily an exception to the popularist flair of Thatcher's administrations. The mechanism of the poll tax is to ensure that everyone who votes in a local election is also involved in paying for the decisions of those ultimately elected. It is an elegant reversal of the no taxation without representation principle. Even in the first poll tax local elections (1990) there were indications that voters, rather than manifesting their dislike of the central legislation, were looking at candidates and parties in a more self-interested way and simply voting for those who were going to cost them the least. In ensuring that there is no representation without taxation the Thatcher government found a powerful popular method of restricting the spending of local authorities. This of itself, of course, will have a profound effect on education. Indeed, as discussed under 'centralization' (see pp. 10–12), it may have a profound effect on the future of LEAs and of local government in England and Wales.

In terms of the Act it is tempting to see the most obvious manifestation of popularism in the National Curriculum. Certainly the back-to-basics emphasis, the stress on regular testing and published results, and the momentum to shift the school curriculum back to the familiar safety of the way things were when the parental, or grandparental, generation were at school, all seem to confirm this. The National Curriculum also contains many nationalist elements (explored in Chapter 2) which place it within this familiar government theme.

There are other aspects to the Act which also derive from and strengthen those fractured aspects of popularism. The mechanisms whereby schools can opt out of LEA control encourage the narrow self-interest of a small group of parents even if this is at the expense of the system as a whole. In the city of Bath where the LEA wished to close one secondary school and create a sixth-form centre in the interests of rationalization, it was possible for that school (Beechen Cliff) to appeal to sectional parental support in order to opt out of LEA control and thereby evade closure. (This was the case which first tested the opting out legislation in the courts; it is further examined in Chapter 4.) Consequently, the LEA (Avon) could not plan education in the city for fear that the next targeted closure victim would also opt out. The LEA's arguments that it could no longer plan rationally in the interests of all the young people in the city were recognized as valid in the High Court when Avon challenged the Secretary of State's judgment on Beechen Cliff:

> The Judge said last summer's decision to allow the school to opt out of Avon control was unlawful because it did not take into account the 'disruption, delay and prolonged uncertainty' it would cause other schools in the city, and ignored the wishes of hundreds of parents who had formally objected to the scheme.
>
> He said: 'there was a failure to have regard to the most important factors, the consequences that the decision would have in terms of time, money, delay and uncertainty for the majority of children in Bath'. (Woodhead *et al.*, 1990)

However, this judgment was overturned when the Lords confirmed that no matter how detrimental to the local planning of schooling a decision by the Secretary of State might be with regard to opting out, he or she has the clear and absolute right to make and enforce such a decision under the terms of the 1988 Act. The further implications of the enforcement of the decision for the city of Bath was that the educational ethos in the city at secondary level was transformed, as fear, uncertainty, planning blight and competitiveness flourished. In this climate, the apparent self-interest of parents as against the interest of the education system as a whole could lead to other applications to opt out from schools that see not their future but their relative status threatened. Popularism successfully appeals to fractional self-interest and indeed elevates it to the key criterion for decision-making.

Privatization

Perhaps privatization should not even be categorized separately from popularism. What superficially may be seen as a short-term strategy of selling off centrally held assets in order temporarily to keep down taxes actually has a longer-term popularist result. Margaret Thatcher acknowledged that privatization had led to electoral support and actually linked this to education: 'Just as we gained great support in the last election from people who had acquired their own homes and shares, so we shall secure still further our political base in 1991/92 by giving people a real say in education and housing' (quoted in Chitty, 1989, p. 221). Those who have brought shares in British Telecom and all the succeeding highly publicized privatizations have bought an interest in the continuation of the party in power lest any other party should seek to renationalize these assets. Similar fears inform the voting patterns of those who have been able to purchase their own council houses. Even more fundamentally, some of these people see themselves as having bought an interest in the capitalist system. The share-holding democrats are proud of their involvement with the large corporations and follow their publicity drives and share prices with equal enthusiasm. The growth of sponsorship in sport and cultural activities, not to mention education, along with the re-found global confidence in capitalism which accompanied the rapid political change in Eastern Europe, have served to make the names and interests of the large corporations a source of derived status for those individuals and groups fractured from any other form of cohesiveness. ADT (the initials in this company's title do not stand for anything, but among its main activities is the provision of private security systems and personnel) are sponsoring a city technology college (CTC) in south London. They are also major sponsors of the London Marathon. Completion of the race, commitment to the college, and loyalty to the corporation will be confused for all those who proudly display the corporation's logo on their tee-shirts.

Opting out into grant-maintained status and the various other changes of school structure (analysed in Chapter 4) have led to a more heterogeneous education system. (It is in order to do full justice to the structural changes that the issue of LMS is discussed twice in this book: firstly, in Chapter 4 to assess the structural implications; secondly, in Chapter 5 to evaluate the detailed implications for schools.) City technology colleges and grant-maintained schools (GMSs) provide the structural forms of privatization within the education system. The newly independent colleges and polytechnics with their expensive corporate logos and their happy enthusiasm for managerial language ('strategic plan', 'chief executive', 'bidding', cost centres', 'the discipline of the bottom line' and worse) are further proud flagships of privatization. They are structural arrangements which have parallels with those hospitals taking the opportunity to opt out of their area health authorities or current proposals to privatize the prison service or the benefits system. They are obviously important in the way in which they disrupt and damage the pattern of LEA provision.

But in terms of education, privatization also has an important ideological valency not distinct from the theme of popularism. The attack on education carried on by politicians of both major parties since 1976 (Bash and Coulby, 1989, pp. 3–18) has been an attack on state education. By contrast, the Thatcher governments have appealed to the fee-paying sector as an area of excellence and have strengthened this sector by the establishment and expansion of the Assisted Places scheme. The CTCs and GMSs can market themselves as private, as distinct from and superior to the much-derided state education provided by LEAs. Like the independent colleges and polytechnics they are part of that radiant entrepreneurial world of corporate capitalism.

Preference given by the government to any form of schooling not maintained by an LEA certainly helps to diversify the forms of institutions and thereby encourage competition between them. It also serves persistently to undermine the state system, as any form of schooling is by definition seen as being preferable to that which the vast majority of the nation's children and young people attend. The argument seems to be that since state schooling cannot be private it cannot be good. Whilst some governors and parents may be persuaded by this to opt out, it does little for the status and morale of teachers and pupils who remain in the persistently denigrated LEA sector.

Financial Control

An explicit goal of the Thatcher administrations was to reduce public expenditure. Less explicit is that this ambition seems to apply to all areas of government activity except those concerned with the armed forces or the administration of law and order. Whilst it may be argued that the Thatcher administrations have actually been remarkably unsuccessful in keeping down public spending, the effects of financial stringency on LEAs are becoming more visible. Indeed, this stringency began before the 1979 election. In terms of the pay level of teachers, the physical fabric of many schools and their lack of appropriate books and equipment (see Chapter 8), the inadequacy of public spending on education is increasingly noticeable.

The implementation of the 1988 Act has led to increases in public expenditure on education which contradict the government's overall fiscal policy. Chapters 2 and 3 show the ways in which the financing of the National Curriculum, especially following the impact of the influential Task Group on Assessment and Testing Report (TGAT, 1987) on its implementation, are rapidly growing whilst still remaining inadequate for the job. The cost of the National Curriculum exercise with its cascade of glossy paper and its associated testing mechanisms – running into millions even at the pilot stage – and the as yet unacknowledged implications for systematic nation-wide in-service training (INSET) are beginning to emerge. Similarly, the costs to the public purse of the creation of the CTCs is now proving to be difficult to justify (Chitty, 1989, pp. 223–4). Some of these costs may be met by shifting resources from other areas of expenditure. For instance, the implementation of the National Curriculum will become a priority for the already allocated expenditure of central government resources on INSET. Nevertheless, additional real costs are beginning to mount and this is one of the reasons for the continuing opposition from some sections of the Cabinet to the establishment of a new national testing bureaucracy (see Chapter 3).

The Act not only contradicts this theme of government policy by increasing expenditure on education; it also, in at least one important respect, completely undermines another strand of policy which could have led to savings in education. As mentioned above, the ability of individual schools to opt out of LEA control has paralysed planning and rationalization of schools. The pressure, not least from the Audit Commission, to save money through the reorganization of (especially secondary) schools has thus been undermined. Since government policy on education is to encourage the majority of schools to opt out, this contradiction in financial policy is to be continued and exacerbated.

It may then be speculated that the government's stress on reducing public expenditure is by no means a purely fiscal measure. Not only are the cuts confined to particular areas of government policy, even within an expensive area of social provision such as education, but also the government is happy to contradict its own financial policies provided the ideological and political gains are sufficiently high. For example, it has been claimed by the Opposition spokesperson on education that CTCs are currently receiving eighty times the funding of LEA-maintained schools (Bates, 1990). Similarly generous capital grants to GMS schools, combined with support from local business, can enhance the sense of independence of these schools and gave the pupils and their parents a sense of identification with a differentiated education system. Meanwhile, commercial sponsorship of both CTCs and GMS schools, along with a more general reliance on parents for voluntary contributions towards school equipment and activities, undermines the sense of free and adequate state education as a universal right and endorses the Thatcherite notion of charity as an appropriate form of resourcing for social and educational provision for the non-privileged. Privatization (see pp. 7–9) may be more about gaining votes than saving money, but it also carried for the Thatcher administrations the force of a moral crusade. It is only by considering the move towards centralization in government policy that the nature of the ideological and political gains can be fully understood.

Centralization

The tendency to shift power to Westminster was an ongoing but undeclared policy of the Thatcher administrations. This focus on Westminster control is actually easiest to recognize with regard to relations with other potential power centres. The refusal to offer even limited devolution to Scotland and Wales is one dimension of this. The xenophobic response to the consolidation of the European Community (EC) is another. The Thatcher government was prepared neither to devolve power to regional assemblies nor willingly to play its part in the emergent European state, presumably because it wished as much power and control as possible to remain at Westminster – that is, with itself.

The abolition of the Greater London Council (GLC), the metropolitan councils and, under the 1988 Act, of the Inner London Education Authority (ILEA) are more substantial manifestations of this policy of centralization. Certainly, these abolitions can more readily be seen as the elimination of powerful and prestigious political opposition. But beyond this is the implication that the local state is no longer a valid entity. The creation of the small inner London borough LEAs is only likely to enhance the impression of the lack of viability of the local administration of social policy (see Chapter 6).

Central control over the extent of local taxation is another important manifestation of the centralizing tendency. The poll tax–capping arrangements are, on the one hand, a systematic development of the previous rate-capping policy. On the other hand, the way that they have been developed and implemented breaks new ground. The formula devised for the first round of poll tax–capping was such as to exclude all Conservative-controlled councils from its rigours. Again it is possible to see this as another side-swipe at political opposition. In this respect it is certainly effective: it makes those councils' tasks in the administration of social policy all the more difficult and at the same time it sends a clear signal to those local electorates that these are 'high-spending' councils, the re-election of which they might wish to consider with care. (The contradiction of this policy with the full implementation of the 1988 Act with its need for additional resources is apparent.) Beyond this, however, poll tax–capping sends a clear signal to all local government that ultimate control rests with Westminster. Local authorities no longer have the right to risk their electoral popularity against high local taxation and high-quality educational and social provision. They cannot take their decision to spend high on education and other areas of social policy to the local electorate or, if they do, central government may overrule the decision of this electorate by imposing poll tax–capping. The poll tax not only attempts to shift local electoral preference towards frugal/parsimonious government (see 'Popularism', pp. 4–7), it also allows the central government to reject the results of local elections, in terms of spending plans, if it so wishes. The mechanism of the poll tax and its associated capping is not an increase in local control but an attempt to restrain local authorities via the electorate, combined with draconian central powers for when a local electorate does not endorse the central government.

It is against this background that the expansion of grant-maintained schools (GMSs) can best be understood. The major item of activity and expenditure for local authorities is education. The 1988 Act removed from them the control of the higher education colleges and polytechnics. LEAs' role in further education had gradually been diminished through the power of the Training Agency. The newly established Training and Enterprise Councils (TECs) have replaced the Training Agency and they have even greater powers and resources in FE decision-making as against LEAs. FE colleges, like the polytechnics before them, may soon be removed from LEA control. The role of the LEAs will be further reduced through the new management arrangements introduced under the Act (see Chapter 7). As increasing numbers of schools opt out into GMS status, the responsibilities of LEAs will diminish further and their resourcing from central government will also be accordingly reduced. It may be that the role of local government in educational provision is being eroded to the point where its only important function will be to monitor the National Curriculum and in particular the testing procedures and results. Any government attempting to lessen the poll tax burden by shifting teacher salaries from local to central government responsibility is likely to exacerbate this trend. The point of erosion of the role of LEAs may still be some years hence, but in the progress towards it there will come a point at which the need for local government itself is questioned. A prefecture system of administrating centrally made policies and decisions may well be seen to be more cost-effective.

EDUCATION POLICY-MAKING AND THE 1988 ACT

So profound are the changes introduced by the Act that there is a danger that it will induce myopia in the commentators. It is difficult to look either back to before the formulation of the 1987 Bill or forward to the point where alternative educational policies will need to be determined. Whilst the government certainly succeeded in stealing the initiative from those LEAs which, in the mid-1980s, were dominating the educational agenda in England and Wales with their anti-racist and anti-sexist policies (see Bash and Coulby, 1989, Chapter 1), there is a danger in assuming that education was in a state of perfection before the Bill came along and ruined everything. This is far from the case. On the one hand, there was much that was wrong with education in England and Wales in 1987 (Bash and Coulby, 1989; Bash *et al.*, 1985) and, on the other hand, not everything in the Act can be dismissed as politically motivated destructiveness. To put this another way, commentators must resist the temptation to become reactionaries, advocating a return to the idealized educational past of the mid-1970s. To comment critically on the Act, as the following chapters frequently do, is not in any sense to suggest that its total repeal would in any way bring about educational utopia. Certainly, alternative policies in many areas of education are urgently needed, and ways forward on these are suggested in the following chapters. But these would need to take account of the failures and tensions within the education system which themselves helped to give rise to the 1988 Act. There can be no pretence that these were not tangible, both within the system and to parents and the electorate.

The other way in which concentration on the Act can induce myopia is that it tempts the commentator to look only at those areas of education which the Act has changed. Certainly these are far from inconsiderable. But areas such as nursery education, the curriculum of higher education, adult education and the whole provision for 16- to 19-year-olds are left effectively untouched by the Act. They are none the less important areas of educational policy and, in the case of 16 to 19 at least, areas where change is urgently needed. They must not sink from the awareness of commentators simply because they are not subject to the excitement of rapid change which is evident in the rest of the system. Areas of educational policy that have been marginalized by the implementation of the Act – and policies directed towards greater educational equality are important in this respect – also need to be brought back to appropriate priority.

Having taken the Act through Parliament, Kenneth Baker left its implementation to his successor John MacGregor.

Fortunately, the new Secretary of State did not attempt to make a short-term political reputation for himself by changing the few things in the system which the Act had left unscathed. He acknowledged the implementation of the 1988 Act to be his priority, as did Kenneth Clarke when he, in turn, took over at Elizabeth House. The implementation of the Act has taken the form of a tidal wave of documentation. The paperwork from the DES, the NCC, SEAC, the curriculum Working Groups and the LEAs, as they all attempted to bring the new structural, political, administrative, financial, curricular and assessment arrangements into place by tight deadlines, was overwhelming. Much of it is referred to in the following chapters. Whether MacGregor saw this paper deluge as bringing about his predecessor's aims or drowning them in detail and complexity was an open question. There were indications, however, that he was aware of the magnitude of the task and of the nature of his inheritance from his predecessor. His short period of tenure at the DES was taken by many to result from his lack of total commitment to the 1988 Act.

REFERENCES

• Bash, L., Coulby, D. and Jones, C. (1985) *Urban Schooling: Theory and Practice*. London: Cassell.
• Bash, L. and Coulby, D. (1989) *The Education Reform Act: Competition and Control*. London: Cassell.
• Bates, S. (1990) Government spending '80 times higher' at city colleges. *Guardian*, 31 August, p. 2.
• Chitty, C. (1989) *Towards a New Education System: The Victory of the New Right?* London: Falmer.
• Task Group on Assessment and Testing (1987) *A Report*. London: DES.
• Woodhead, S., Ashton, G., Symington, D., Best, W. and Thomas, M. (1990) Education Secretary told: re-do homework. *(Bath) Evening Chronicle*, 24 February, p. 1.

2
The National Curriculum

David Coulby

THE POLITICAL CURRICULUM

So extensive are the powers given to the Secretary of State for Education and Science with regard to the school curriculum by the 1988 Act, that it would seem as if there were almost no room for conflict. The Secretary of State appoints the individual members of both the National Curriculum Council (NCC) and the School Examinations and Assessment Council (SEAC). Their membership is in no sense meant to represent particular interest groups within education and beyond. Individual members have no constituency such as trade unions or local education authorities (LEAs) which might be politically opposed to the Secretary of State. They are appointed in their own personal capacity. In practice this has meant that people from education and beyond certainly are included but they have no appeal to, or mandate from, any external group. It has also meant that people on these two Councils who hold vocal political views different from those of the Secretary of State are rather hard to find. Exactly the same could be said of the curriculum Working Groups (WGs). Their memberships are appointed in a personal capacity, many of their members being widely respected either in terms of their subject discipline or in general educational terms; people whose views might be radical or lead to conflict are conspicuous by their absence. Indeed, in the second half of 1990 when it was becoming clear that Secretary of State MacGregor was reversing many of his predecessor's decisions on the National Curriculum (see pp. 21–5), he was able to forestall criticism from within his own party by making notably right-wing appointments to fill vacancies on both the NCC and SEAC.

The 1988 Act has, then, apparently set up the machinery of consensus for the Secretary of State. Groups of people with convergent political opinions, none of them representative of outside interests and each appropriately grateful for the patronage of the Secretary of State, might be expected to arrive, without too much tension, at views not entirely dissimilar from those of the person who appointed them. Lest there should be any doubt that this is what is intended – and it is difficult to see how there could be – the Secretary of State has provided each WG with extensive and clear advice both before and during the process of establishing the Attainment Targets (ATs), Profile Components (PCs) and Programmes of Study. Just in case anything untoward were to occur during the process of determining the school curriculum within any subject area, it is clear in the 1988 Act that all this apparatus – WGs, NCC, SEAC – is anyway only advisory to the Secretary of State who may, if so minded, disregard all advice and follow political or personal inclinations. Perhaps it was some awareness of this that prompted former Conservative Prime Minister Edward Heath to comment, whilst the Bill was before Parliament, that 'The Secretary of State has taken more powers under the Bill than any other member of the Cabinet, more than my right honourable friends the Chancellor of the Exchequer, the Secretary of State for Defence and the Secretary of State for Social Services' (quoted in Wragg, 1988, p. 16). The centralized control, which in many respects is one of the crucial dimensions of the 1988 Act, would seem to have left little institutional space for conflict over the school curriculum.

In the event this was not the case and press reports indicate that the debates within the WGs, and between the WGs, the NCC, and the Secretaries of State for Education and Science have often been intense, bitter and laden with political content. The minutes of these Working Groups have not been made public nor have those of the conversations between the various Chairs and the Secretary of State. These Working Groups were actually having the definitive conversations about the content of school knowledge in England and Wales and their minutes would make interesting reading for more than those concerned with the politics of the implementation of the 1988 Act. A group of people were convened to decide what should be the content of the subjects taught in primary and secondary schools. It is possible that in their debates the clarity and simplicity of political intentions encountered the complexity of professional practice. Their debates also might well have reflected familiar conflicts within each subject area, but the resolution of those debates constituted an unprecedented (if faintly ludicrous) step towards the finalization of school knowledge. There were surprisingly few leaks from the Groups, and it would be interesting to know their mode of procedure and especially whether they split up into sub-groups to determine particular PCs or ATs. If this were the procedure it might explain the resulting proliferation of PCs and ATs (see 'The overcrowded curriculum', pp. 21-5). Perhaps the Chairs of the Working Groups, beset with demands for the inclusion of material from a range of sub-groups, took the easy route and simply included everything.

Examples of the conflicts which did occur can be taken from the two WGs with perhaps the most controversial jobs to do: English and History. Whilst the Education Bill was still before Parliament a Committee of Inquiry into the Teaching of English Language had been established. The reasons for this were the orchestration of traditionalist fears over changes in the language curriculum which had supposedly resulted in matters such as grammar and spelling being neglected at both primary and secondary school. Given that this committee, chaired by Kingman, was already in operation, it was thought inappropriate to establish a working group. The Kingman Report (DES, 1988) made recommendations which could be interpreted as a reassertion of the importance of grammar in the English curriculum. When a delighted Secretary of State for Education and Science (then Baker) affirmed that the Kingman Report should form the basis for the deliberations of the English Working Group, and announced that the Group would be chaired by Professor Brian Cox, a member of the Kingman Committee and prominent Black Paperist, fears about the politicization of the school curriculum were at their highest.

Because of the scramble to have the primary core curriculum up and running in September 1989, the English Working Group published its recommendations for ages 5 to 11 (DES and Welsh Office, 1988) in advance of completing its work on the secondary phase (DES and Welsh Office, 1989a). There was no interim report, Kingman perhaps being perceived to have done that job. The Final Reports did not, in the event, echo the traditionalist concerns of Kingman, advocating instead the adoption of much of the best of current progressive practice in the language area, including speaking and listening and the recognition of the importance of non-standard forms of English and of the strengths of bilingual pupils. With the September 1989 deadline for the introduction of the core curriculum to 5-year-olds ever nearer, the NCC followed up with ATs and Programmes of Study for the first key stage only (NCC, 1989a). In this case the NCC's changes apparently showed them to be more traditionalist than the government. It was reported in the press at the time that Cox and his entire Working Group had threatened to resign, leaving their secondary work uncompleted, because of the changes made by the NCC (Nash, 1989). In the event the then Secretary of State, Baker, sided with Cox and the Final Orders for the primary phase (DES and Welsh Office, 1989b) actually saw the reinstatement of the more liberal and professionally acceptable consensus advocated by the Working Group.

The Final Orders for the secondary phase proved more contentious. The Secretary of State cut out all the Working Group's references to reading from a range of cultures. Nash gives some idea of the magnitude of the resulting conflict: 'The deletions have drawn strong condemnation from Professor Brian Cox, the chairman [*sic*] of the working group, and from the Commission for Racial Equality. Opposition MPs and English teachers have also joined the attack' (Nash, 1990, p. A1). The *Times Educational Supplement* (TES) in an uncharacteristically critical leader, commented that 'the Government, in its resistance to multi-cultural approaches, is simply demonstrating its suspicion of other cultures in general' (TES, 1990, p. A23). The then Minister of State, Angela Rumbold, attempted to allay these fears in a letter to the TES (Rumbold, 1990, p. A17), but with little success. The impression of political interference to support a 'whites-only' view of literature persisted. A subsequent contributor to the correspondence not only persists with the conflict but rightly notes where, on this issue, the ultimate power resides:

it is necessary to challenge Mrs Rumbold's assertion that consultation is a two way process, whereas we have seen throughout the implementation of the Education Reform Act that the consultation process consists of the Secretary of State seeking views on proposals and then choosing either to listen or not to listen to those views, however great their strength or unanimity. In this particular case, it is worth noting that the National Curriculum Council in its report on the consultation process, quite clearly recommended the inclusion of texts from other cultures within both the programmes of study and the statements of attainment. (Bibby, 1990, 23)

The wider implications of the ethnocentrism reflected in this decision of the Secretary of State are discussed in the section on 'The nationalist curriculum' (see pp. 30-7).

It had been predicted (Bash and Coulby, 1989) that History was the school subject the finalization of which was most likely to generate political interference and conflict. In the event this was proved to be the case. John MacGregor had replaced the self-styled historian Kenneth Baker as Secretary of State by the time the History WG made its Interim Report (History Working Group, 1989). His response, however, was all that the architect of the 1988 Act might have wished. He indicated that he wanted more time to be spent on British history; he wished for explicit historical knowledge to be included in the ATs; he placed a clear stress on chronology and he invited them in their final report to spell out the 'content of knowledge – including dates, events and people – that must be taught to pupils' (History Working Group, 1989, no page number at this point in their text). An ethnocentric history curriculum stressing facts rather than analysis was certainly the closest the National Curriculum had come, at that stage, to being party political.

Political interference was also at its most blatant with regard to this subject. Prior to the publication of the Working Group's Final Report, the then Prime Minister herself seems to have intervened:

> The long-overdue final report of the national curriculum history working group has failed to win Government support after a top-level meeting between Mr John MacGregor, the Education Secretary, and the Prime Minister, Mrs Thatcher, whose close involvement with the progress of the history curriculum has led to Opposition accusations of 'constitutional impropriety', is understood to be dissatisfied with the report, despite the group's efforts to give British history a more central role. (Nash and Darking, 1990, p. 1)

Whilst 'constitutional impropriety' might indicate a failure to understand where the 1988 Act has placed curricular powers, this partisan writing of the school curriculum is an exercise in Whig history which would have made Macaulay envious. When the Working Group's Final Report was published (History Working Group, 1990), it did not meet with quite the general academic and professional disdain which had greeted their earlier effort, despite the fact that they had gone some way towards meeting the Secretary of State's demands. Despite the WG's efforts to please the government, a procedure was introduced which had not been deemed necessary for the subjects which had reported earlier. The Secretary of State allowed two further months for public discussion before the Final Report went forward to be discussed by the NCC. Following this discussion Secretary of State MacGregor made his own subtle intervention in the reworking of the WG's proposals (DES, 1990). This intervention is discussed on pp. 30-7 in the section entitled 'The nationalist curriculum', where it is shown that it was mainly European and world history which he excised from the National Curriculum. He also reasserted his views about the importance of knowledge, making it a part of the pre-eminent AT. Whilst the WG's proposals probably did need to be slimmed down, it is not hard to discern the assertion of political criteria in these revisions. The NCC worked further on the proposals, but the last word on Whig history was with Kenneth Clarke, who had taken over as Secretary of State in time to intervene in the Final Orders. He insisted these followed his own view that history ended in the 1960s and that events thereafter constitute current affairs, which should not form part of the National Curriculum. His total disregard of previous advice and consultation demonstrated the political - almost personal - control which the Secretary of State now exerts over the curriculum.

There are important issues here with regard to History as a subject and many of these are taken up in the section entitled 'The nationalist curriculum'. The more general issue concerns the political determination of school knowledge and the arrangements the 1988 Act makes to arbitrate conflict in this area. By giving all power to the Secretary of State the risk is established of a politically partisan school curriculum in areas other than History. Any Secretary of State with a claim, no matter how feeble, to subject expertise may choose to become involved in what is taught in schools. The case of History indicates the extent to which the entire school curriculum is open to political and politicized interference. The danger here is twofold: firstly, that of school knowledge being blatantly politically biased; secondly, the school curriculum could become frozen in time as a Secretary of State, without a recent or comprehensive grounding in a subject, insists that it be taught in the way in which it was when he or she was at school. Clarke's belated but crucial interventions, in geography as well as history, demonstrate the authority given to the Secretary of State's political views and personal whims.

THE OVERCROWDED CURRICULUM

One of the results of dividing the school curriculum into subjects and then establishing WGs to determine the content of each was to place stress on the actual time available within the school day. A panel of experts in a field is likely to consider that their particular area is important and needs plenty of school time; it is likely to do this overtly, by making demands on timetable time, or covertly, by listing such a large number of ATs that they can only be covered in a considerable amount of time. Since the ultimate political arbiters seem to favour knowledge rather than skills, the tendency toward the compilation of lengthy lists is further encouraged. Furthermore, both the 1988 Act and the statements from the three Secretaries of State for Education and Science have fought shy of saying how much school time should be spent on either the entire National Curriculum or on specific subjects. The WGs have thus seen school time as being something they are able to play for.

The Science Working Group got this process off to a splendid start with their bid for 20 per cent of secondary school time. In the event this bid was only partially successful. Science has, however, under the auspices of the National Curriculum, established itself as deserving much more time at both primary and secondary levels. In doing this, Science has both set an example which others may wish to follow and squeezed the amount of school time for which the remaining subjects must compete among themselves. This competition between subject areas seems to be resulting in a proliferation of ATs to the extent where, especially at primary level, the practicality of the whole National Curriculum enterprise seems to be in danger.

Rather than helping with this difficulty, a recent intervention from the NCC (NCC, 1990) seems likely to seriously exacerbate it. The NCC's approach is actually to fill the school curriculum with yet more apparatus and material in terms of 'dimensions', 'skills' and 'themes'. The dimensions advocated by the NCC would find an enthusiastic supporter in the current writer: 'Dimensions such as a commitment to providing equal opportunities for all pupils, and a recognition that preparation for life in a multi-cultural society is relevant to all pupils should permeate every aspect of the curriculum' (NCC, 1990, p. 2). There would seem to be some tension between this recommendation and Secretary of State MacGregor's approval of the Final Orders for English or his response to the History WG's Interim Report (both discussed on pp. 30–7). Again, under 'skills', which the NCC illustrates as 'communication, numeracy, study, problem solving, personal and social, information technology' (NCC, 1990, p. 3), it is difficult to do other than to agree with gratitude. Reservations arise only at the tone in which this advice is offered: 'The National Curriculum Council considers it absolutely essential that these skills are fostered across the whole curriculum in a measured and planned way' (NCC, 1990, p. 3). Further well-meant advice on what needs to be fostered in a measured and planned way was precisely what schools did not need in 1990.

Under the 'themes', the curricular proliferation is even more obvious. According to the NCC, these include economic and industrial understanding, careers education and guidance, health education, education for citizenship, environmental education (NCC, 1990, pp. 4–6). Even more worrying is that this is 'by no means a conclusive list' (p. 4) so teachers and heads can expect further grey booklets with supplementary 'themes'. It is not that these themes are undesirable, it is rather that if they are so undeniably desirable then it should be the business of the NCC to see that they are appropriately represented in the Final Orders for those subject areas where they can be appropriately covered. Instead, the whole difficulty of curricular intelligibility seems to be in the process of being shifted from the WGs and the NCC down to the schools and teachers. The NCC seem to be acknowledging that the emerging National Curriculum is incomplete and unintelligible but, instead of halting the process until something altogether more considered can be done, it is asking the schools to resolve those issues which the people involved in the political determination of school knowledge had ignored, misunderstood or botched. In fairness to the NCC it should be noted that the recommendations in *The Whole Curriculum* were not something which it dreamed up as its own alternative to the National Curriculum. Most of the points raised by the NCC had already been stressed by the DES in the widely circulated *National Curriculum: From Policy to Practice* (DES, 1989, especially section 3). Nevertheless, if there was no conflict there was certainly confusion.

At this point, the National Curriculum consisted of nine subjects at primary school and ten at secondary school (except in Wales where there are ten and eleven respectively); if Religious Education (RE) is included, this makes ten at primary and eleven at secondary school (with eleven and twelve respectively in Wales). Each of these subjects either has or will have a varying number of Profile Components and an equally varying but different number of Attainment Targets; each subject is to have ten levels and is to be taught to pupils across four key stages; across these nine, ten, eleven or twelve subjects are to be taught an indeterminate number of 'dimensions', at least six 'skills' and certainly more than five 'themes'. When Lord Joseph was Secretary of State for Education and Science he was highly critical of the school curriculum because it contained too much 'clutter'.

The next chapter outlines the many difficulties which the acceptance of the recommendations of the Report of the Task Group on Assessment and Testing (TGAT) posed for the national testing arrangements. The acceptance of the Report (Task Group on Assessment and Testing, 1987) also had important implications for the shape of the National Curriculum itself. Following the model of graded tests, which had proved helpful in the teaching of Mathematics and foreign languages, TGAT recommended that all National Curriculum subjects should be structured into ten levels, each to correspond to a year of schooling. This is indeed the shape which the National Curriculum subjects have followed. The levels are of gradual difficulty to follow the development of pupils as they mature and progress. This structure is based on the presumption that all the subjects are organized hierarchically, that is that one element of the subject logically comes before another. It is assumed that the easier fundamentals can be taught first to younger children, thereby providing the basis for older pupils to go on to the more complex and difficult dimensions of the subject. This may be the case for subjects such as Mathematics or foreign languages, or, if it is not the case for the nature of the subjects themselves, it may still be helpful to teach them in this way, but it is hardly the case for other subjects such as History or Geography. If certain places, topics or periods are taught only to young children, then the hierarchical organization would imply that these subjects are somehow simpler. Pupils might then leave school with only a 6-year-old's understanding of India, or the water cycle, or the seventeenth century.

The hierarchical organization of school subjects into ten levels disregards the structure and organization of particular disciplines. It is also another source of the overcrowding of the National Curriculum. Once the ten levels were established as a template for all the subject WGs, they could not opt for a more gradual progression nor for very much repetition. Certainly any possibility that they might suggest that their subject did not need to be every pupil's priority in every year of compulsory schooling was eradicated. The structure of the National Curriculum encouraged them to include large amounts of material rather than to opt for a judicious selection across ten years. Perhaps if the WGs had been based on the phases of children's development rather than on subject disciplines, this overcrowding might have been avoided.

The overcrowded curriculum points to the contradiction between the simplicity of Baker's model of a National Curriculum entitlement for all children and young people from 5 to 16 and the complexity of the school knowledge which schools, parents and employers wish to be available. There is not enough time in school for everyone to take everything, even when everything is constrained within the National Curriculum framework. This contradiction gradually became more alarming with particular regard to the curriculum and assessment of young people at key stage 4. Without any pattern of options or specialisms, there would be no space for pupils to take subjects which Secretary of State MacGregor thought desirable – Economics, Classics, a second modern language or three separate sciences – but which unfortunately were not within his predecessor's framework. His request to NCC, in the summer of 1990, that they re-examine the curriculum framework for the 14 to 16 phase and that they consider the possibility of only the core subjects plus technology and a modern foreign language being compulsory for all, is a retreat from the terms of the 1988 Act so significant that it may ultimately require amending legislation. Despite NCC advice this was the decision ultimately taken by his successor, Clarke. The concept of an entitlement curriculum was thus abandoned for the 14 to 16 phase. Ironically, resistance to flexibility at this phase actually came from the secondary headteachers. The National Curriculum framework at least provided them with a simple structure in a curriculum phase which appeared to be becoming ever more complex (St John-Brooks, 1990). Clarke's decision means that the 14 to 16 curriculum may again be split into two tiers, of high-status academic subjects and low-status vocational subjects.

THE OUTDATED CURRICULUM

The resemblance of the National Curriculum to the old-fashioned grammar school curriculum has already been noted and explored (Bash and Coulby, 1989, Chapter 4). What is worth briefly emphasizing here is the persistent contradiction between this view of the school curriculum and other areas of government policy on education. The conflict is with the importance which government departments other than the DES place on the two areas of technology and enterprise.

The Department of Employment formed a view of the needs of employers in respect of training which was partly derived from the high and mounting youth unemployment of the early 1980s (Bash *et al.*, 1985, Chapter 7). Under the auspices of the Manpower Services Commission (MSC) (which subsequently became the Training Agency, and is now abolished) the Department established a sequence of initiatives, initially for young school leavers, of which the Youth Training Scheme (YTS) was the most enduring. The aim of YTS courses was to provide young people with skills, including social skills, which, after eleven years of schooling, they were apparently still lacking. The whole YTS initiative could be seen as a critique of formal schooling and particularly of the secondary school curriculum. Behind it lay the fallacy that youth unemployment in the UK was caused by a shortage of skills rather than a lack of investment in industry (Bash *et al.*, 1985, Chapter 7). Nevertheless, quite explicit within the rationale of YTS were some progressive curricular ideas.

The most obvious of these was the stress on equal opportunities, especially in terms of gender. The YTS also stressed the acquisition of technological skills and, more problematically, of an enterprising attitude (the concept of enterprise is discussed on pp. 27–8). Under the YTS scheme some further education colleges were able to pioneer the development of profiling and records of achievement (for the progress of which initiative see Chapter 3).

In 1982 the Department of Employment, again through the MSC, introduced the Technical and Vocational Education Initiative (TVEI). With pilot schemes commencing in 1983, this was aimed not at the post-16 phase but at 14- to 18-year-olds many of whom were still within compulsory schooling. With high funding, selectively targeted, and with similar aims to the YTS scheme, the TVEI had a dramatic impact on secondary schooling in many of the schools and LEAs which were involved. Although initially regarded with distrust by many teachers and by many LEAs which considered themselves to be progressive (for example the Inner London Education Authority), the TVEI proved to have a great potential, particularly in terms of its stress on technological skills and equal opportunities. Some have seen the TVEI as a major blow by the Department of Employment against the DES and it certainly must be regarded as a significant critique by one government department of what was happening within the purview of another. Others have seen the TVEI initiative as having been hijacked by teachers and put to purposes different from or even oppositional to the intentions of its original architects (for a full consideration of this debate see Hickox and Moore, 1990). This hypothesis is more difficult to sustain. During the 1980s all government departments developed great flair for summarily cutting off the funding for any developments of which they did not approve, and it is unlikely that the Department of Employment would have continued to expand a scheme which was actually being developed in ways which were counter to its intentions. Rather, it may be that the progressive opening up of the secondary school curriculum which many schools established under TVEI was actually not far removed from the aspirations of the Department of Employment. If this is the case, then it is important to note that these aspirations have still not been acknowledged by the DES since the principles which informed TVEI – industrial and commercial relevance as well as equal opportunities – are of only marginal importance within the National Curriculum.

The Department of Employment again used the MSC/Training Agency for its well-funded foray into higher education, the Enterprise in Higher Education (EHE) scheme. What needs some clarification here, in order to understand the initiative, is the operationalization of the concept of enterprise. On the surface enterprise appears to be a concept which carries all the overtones of crude competitive capitalism. Margaret Thatcher and Lord Young were two particularly avid exponents of the benefits that 'enterprise' could bring both to the economy and to social and moral values. It would appear to be not only politically suspect, as the ideological property of only one major political party, but also outdated as referring to an earlier form of the organization of capital than that which is currently developing. In practice, within the EHE scheme, the concept of enterprise is being operationalized to include a range of progressive developments including forging closer links with industry and commerce, developing proactive methods of teaching, learning, assessing and recording, and introducing new technology into many areas of the higher education curriculum. Far from being the preserve of a reactionary ideology, it seems that the notion of enterprise may have great potential for important developments in education, particularly when linked, as it is again in this scheme, to selective but high funding. Again it would be a mistake to jump to the conclusion that the results of the scheme are radically different from the intentions of its originators. It may be, rather, that the Department of Employment had a radically different view of education from that encapsulated in the National Curriculum.

A much smaller scheme than YTS, TVEI, or EHE may be briefly mentioned here since it is another example of the ambivalent nature of the concept of enterprise and because it provides an example of a second government department establishing educational priorities in marked contrast to the DES. The Enterprise Awareness in Teacher Education (EATE) scheme was launched by the Department of Trade and Industry (DTI) in 1989. Difficulties with the concept of enterprise were once more encountered, but again the apparently ideologically restrictive terminology did not prevent the encouragement of progressive work. The specifically targeted funding allowed for a two-way interchange between people in teacher education and those in their neighbouring commercial and industrial sector. The resulting widened perceptions on both sides are part of that vital erosion of the barriers between education and the workplace which is disappointingly not helped by the introduction of the National Curriculum with its emphasis on scholarly subjects rather than workplace skills. It has been left to the NCC to revive this aspect of secondary education through emphasis on the appropriate 'themes' and 'skills' (see 'The overcrowded curriculum', pp. 21–5).

The contradiction here is with the aspirations and initiatives of other government departments. The National Curriculum appears to take little note of those schemes which have actually been established by, especially, the Department of Employment, as a response to perceived inadequacies in secondary, further and higher education. A born-again grammar school curriculum is now being implemented (Bash and Coulby, 1989, Chapter 4) as if these initiatives had never occurred. Despite the 1990 extension, the future of TVEI is now in jeopardy following the demise of the Training Agency. The National Curriculum has denied it any central role in the 14 to 16 phase. Certainly the conflict here is between the intentions of various components of the government rather than the outcomes in finalized curriculum terms. The introduction of TVEI, followed by that of the GCSE and now the National Curriculum, has resulted in major uncertainties in the curriculum of the 14 to 16 phase. It may be that these uncertainties cannot be resolved until the issue of post-compulsory education is comprehensively addressed (see Chapter 7). MacGregor's dawning acknowledgement of the difficulties presented to key stage 4 by the full implementation of the National Curriculum, and Clarke's more rapid interventions, may mean that the conflicts are at last to be acknowledged if not resolved.

THE DISINTEGRATED CURRICULUM

The particular inappropriateness of the subject-based National Curriculum to education at primary level has already been noted (Coulby, 1990; Ward, 1990). To the extent that the conflict here is with existing and developing primary practice, it must be taken as the actual intention of the 1988 Act. Interestingly, however, the NCC has attempted to resolve this conflict. *Curriculum Guidance 1: A Framework for the Primary Curriculum* (NCC,

1989b) begins most reassuringly: 'The description of the National Curriculum in terms of foundation subjects is not a description of how the school day should be organised or the curriculum delivered' (p. 1). The booklet then goes on to those other things which the NCC considers to be important but which are not actually in the National Curriculum and which it later identifies as themes, dimensions and skills (see 'The overcrowded curriculum', pp. 21–5).

Although ostensibly a defence of schools' ability to continue working with an integrated curriculum, the document has the greatest difficulty steering between what it regards as good practice and the terms of the legislation which the NCC was actually established to implement: 'Planning under subject headings does not preclude flexibility of delivery across subject boundaries. It may not always make best sense to deliver all subjects in simple strands in a week. The issue, for schools, will be how to combine subject strands in coherent ways' (p. 7). If this is the issue, then has not the National Curriculum framework done little more for primary schools than make things unnecessarily complicated by attempting to untangle threads best left woven together?

In the section on Early Years the document again advocates practice which is actually quite apart from the National Curriculum: 'the opportunity now exists to build on good early years practice to provide: . . . a curriculum which is relevant and enjoyable to the children and draws on their own experiences' (p. 21). It is difficult to see why this aspiration is limited to the early years or how it is anything but hindered by the introduction of the inflexible subject-based National Curriculum. There seems to be a real conflict within the NCC itself as to what is known to be good primary practice and the demands of the National Curriculum.

The main part of the booklet is dominated by the vocabulary of delivery. This metaphor reveals a lot about the National Curriculum and the way in which it is perceived by the NCC. The curriculum is seen as a commodity which can unproblematically be delivered by the NCC via schools and teachers to pupils in schools. The pupils are simply recipients of this delivery, empty vessels (Freire, 1972) which must be crammed as full as possible as quickly as possible with the commodified National Curriculum. This view of the curriculum takes no account that the pupils may not learn what the NCC is so anxious for schools to teach them. Pupils, their backgrounds, motivations, interests, differential learning styles and skills play no part in a curriculum which is to be delivered to them like the daily papers. Since learning is perceived as a one-way process in which pupils provide neither hindrance nor assistance to the unproblematic delivery of the National Curriculum, then the focus of attention is shifted to use of time in the school week in order to maximize the amount that can be delivered.

This obsession with time is a further feature of the *Framework* document. A whole interrogatory section poses such issues as 'how is time used at present? what restrictions are there on using this time for formal curriculum delivery, e.g. assembly, registration, unforeseen accidents/incidents, movement around the school, changing from one activity to another? . . . is it necessary to establish new priorities in the use of time? how will this be done?' (p. 5). Pausing only to note the pompous rewording of teaching as 'formal curriculum delivery' and the strange idea that assembly would be an interruption to this process rather than an integral part of it, a further example may provide an insight into why the NCC's enthusiasm for integration is suffused with this theme of time-management: 'As schools become increasingly familiar with the National Curriculum it will become clear that there are many areas where links between the foundation subjects will lead to effective and efficient use of time' (p. 8). Links will not lead to a more rounded and practical approach to knowledge, they will not help children make academic connections across their disintegrated curriculum, they will not provide interesting and diverse opportunities for learning differentiated according to the pupils' interests: the reason why these links are important is only that they will save time. Could it be that by 1989 the NCC were already recognizing that the National Curriculum was becoming overcrowded? In which case their enthusiasm for an integrated primary curriculum is due mainly to the fact that this was the only way in which they could cram the National Curriculum into the school week for 'delivery' to primary pupils. The enthusiasm for integration is not derived from a sound appreciation of good primary practice but from the need to get a quart into a pint pot.

THE NATIONALIST CURRICULUM

As the National Curriculum emerges, its nationalist character can be detected in at least four subject areas; English, modern foreign languages, History and RE. In some ways the tendency toward nationalism is implicit in the subject-based structure of the National Curriculum, especially given the traditionalist subjects that have been selected for prominence. More integrated thematic approaches such as Global Relations or Health Studies, with an explicit commitment to internationalist, multicultural and anti-racist approaches, were discarded in favour of the traditional grammar school approach. Similarly, the issue with regard to RE is not the product of dialogue and conflict within and between the Working Groups, the NCC and the DES. It is, rather, a matter of explicit statement and intention on the face of the 1988 Act.

The issue of multicultural texts in English has already been mentioned in the section above on the political curriculum. With regard to modern foreign languages the nationalist issue revolves round which language(s) should be taught; in particular what prominence should be given to the heritage languages (mother tongues) of groups within the UK. Prior to the establishment of the Working Group the DES had suggested that there should be a hierarchy of foreign languages. They put forward one list with all the state languages of the European Community (EC) and another list which included other major world languages such as Russian, Chinese, Punjabi and Bengali. The proposal was that secondary schools should teach one of the languages from the first (EC) list. Only if a language from this list were offered could the school additionally teach a language from the second schedule.

The Modern Foreign Languages WG identified the difficulties involved in this approach: 'the two-list format implies a hierarchy of languages, with those in Schedule 2 apparently deemed to be less worthwhile in their own right than those in Schedule 1' (Modern Foreign Languages Working Group, 1990, p. 145). This hierarchy is all the more unfortunate in that many of the important heritage languages in England and Wales, such as Turkish or Bengali, are seen to be in the inferior category. The WG, however, only pay lip service to the importance of heritage languages:

> In deciding which languages to offer, schools should have regard to the wishes of parents, and bilingual pupils should wherever possible be given the opportunity to study a

> language new to them. However, we believe that, as now,
> there should be no restriction on bilingual pupils studying
> the language of their home or community as their first
> foreign language ... (pp. 145-6)

The Report does not show sufficient respect for the language
skills of bilingual pupils; it does not recognize that many of
the languages they speak are world languages with economic,
political and cultural significance far beyond the EC; it does not
see the potential for monoglot English-speaking pupils to learn
one of the non-EC heritage languages of England and Wales
which might actually be one of the prominent languages in the
city where they live. The interim recommendation, then, actually
retains the hierarchy of languages only in a less blatant form:

> we believe that each pupil must be offered the opportunity
> of choosing to study a working language of the EC to meet
> the National Curriculum modern foreign language require-
> ments. Thus if a school offers only one foreign language for
> pupils aged 11-16, that language would have to be an EC
> working language. If a school offers those children two
> foreign languages one would have to be an EC working
> language, and the other might be a non-EC language; pupils
> could then choose to study the non-EC language as their
> foreign language foundation subject within the National
> Curriculum. (p. 145)

It might be thought that to describe this as nationalist is
stretching the point rather far. The Modern Foreign Languages
WG is prioritizing the international EC in a way which is appropriate to the political position of the UK at the end of the twentieth century. The UK's ambiguous attitude to the EC is referred
to later in this section. At this stage, however, a more cynical
exegesis of the WG's recommendation can be offered. All schools
will have to teach a nice safe 'white' foreign language like French
or German. Schools will be allowed to teach 'black' foreign
languages like Bengali, but only if they also have a 'white' foreign
language on offer. There will thus be no possibility of white
children finding themselves in a school where the only foreign
language on offer is a 'black' one. Thus, the compulsory National
Curriculum modern foreign language requirement of the 1988
Act would not be able to be used to compel a white child to

study a 'black' language. To call this nationalist or racist might be stretching the point too far, but it is certainly representative of the neo-assimilationist policies which characterized the third Thatcher government and it certainly means that the racism of children and their parents will never be confronted by the languages they are compelled to learn within the National Curriculum.

The case for nationalism within National Curriculum History needs less careful arguing. It is appropriate to examine the History WG's proposals (History Working Group, 1990) in some detail as this is the National Curriculum subject most vulnerable to political interpretation and partisan bias. The way in which a school system presents the history of the nation state will carry messages about sensitive subjects such as religion, class structures, patterns of inequality and foreign relations. It is doubtful if a non-political presentation of history is possible since the subject may be seen as political by definition, but it is reasonable to aspire to a comprehensive and many-sided approach. As discussed in 'The political curriculum', MacGregor's early interventions were explicitly to try to get the WG to include more British (and therefore, less international) history within the curriculum. The apparent Eurocentrism of the Modern Foreign Languages WG is displaced by the more familiar Anglocentrism (see pp. 34–5 for the place of the rest of the UK in British history). The implications of this are far reaching; they extend to pupils' perceptions of the UK itself, the EC, global relations and the position of black people in UK schools and society. This section goes on to examine these four implications in turn.

It is clear that the History WG attempted to address the place of non-English history in British history (History Working Group, 1990). In terms of concrete proposals their efforts centred on History Study Unit (HSU) 15 for key stage 3 'The Making of the United Kingdom: c. 1500 to c. 1750' and HSU 19 also for key stage 3 'Culture and Society in Ireland up to early C20th'. The actual inclusion of these two units must itself be seen as an important attempt to break down the Anglocentric view of history. Although the details of the proposals may be disappointing, the structure is there for teachers to fill in the details and to provide a view of history which counters English triumphalism. Although HSU 19 was swept away by Secretary of State MacGregor's streamlining of the proposals, HSU 15 (pp. 62–3) remained and does not shy away from some of the unpleasant incidents: 'Ulster Plantation, 1641 rising, massacres of Drogheda and Wexford'. It does not suggest any examination of the essentially colonial status of Ireland and the Irish. Furthermore, despite going through to 1750 there is no mention of Culloden and the suppression of the Highlands. Significantly the 'Glorious Revolution' is mentioned twice – once with inverted commas and once without.

In terms of developing pupils' perceptions of those countries comprising the EC, there are certainly a range of proposed HSUs which address this, including 'Britain and the Great War: 1914 to 1918'; 'Reformation and religious diversity in Western Europe in C16th'; 'The Italian Renaissance'; 'The French Revolution and the Napoleonic era'; 'The era of the Second World War: 1933–1948'; 'East and West: Europe 1948 to the present day' (p. 33). Again, all but the latter two were swept away in Secretary of State MacGregor's streamlining. The present day was pushed back to the 1960s by Clarke. Since only the Second World War HSU is compulsory, the Secretaries of State have given schools the ability to opt out of more European content in History. Furthermore, even within the WG's proposals what was lacking was the sense of the interactions within European history. There was little sense of movement and influence within European states, between them and with countries beyond them. The question is to do with the nature of the perception of the EC which the National Curriculum will try to develop in pupils. Will it be a sense of interacting forces and movements – political, cultural, demographic, economic – across Europe and beyond or will it be a sequence of decontextualized great men (for such is the paradigm) and events? The latter option was very much to the forefront for the History WG, and the subsequent stages in the finalization of the National Curriculum for History have only enforced this trend.

The History WG's final proposals did contain substantial elements of non-European history: these include HSUs on Islamic civilization, Imperial China, India 1526 to 1805, five units on America, units on the recent history of India and Pakistan, Africa south of the Sahara, and on Japan and China. This is an impressively wide coverage and even the undue concentration on America is mitigated by the fact that one of the units is on 'native peoples' and another on 'black peoples'. However, the units on Islamic civilization, China, India and four of the five American units were excised in Secretary of State MacGregor's revisions. Sensitive to the overcrowded nature of the school curriculum discussed above, MacGregor sensibly slimmed down the WG's proposals. Especially at key stage 3 and for young people not taking GCSE History at key stage 4, the reduction in content is substantial. Furthermore, by giving schools the flexibility to develop more of their own units the Secretary of State's revisions lift the weight of the WG's edifice. In the process, of course, the whole point of the National Curriculum, in terms of national continuity and coherence of learning, was endangered.

In the purge of HSUs 18 to 31, it was mainly non-English and non-British history which suffered. The first time that a Secretary of State has intervened to give schools more flexibility in the National Curriculum, it has been to give them the freedom not to teach so much European and world history. Even in the WG's final proposals, what was missing – at least for the modern period – was any notion of a world system. History was still described largely in terms of isolated nation states and the nation states chosen are mostly those that have achieved historical or contemporary political/economic dominance. The notable exception here was HSU 38, 'Africa south of the Sahara since 1945', an optional unit for key stage 4. Although focusing only on territories that were once under British rule, the essential and exemplary information includes: 'Apartheid; resistance; changes'; 'Food and cash crops. World Markets . . . International loans and debts'; 'New music. Novels. Film industry. Sport and athletics'. This unit, actually incorporated in the final orders, would allow older pupils the opportunity to understand some of contemporary African history within the world economic system and to gain some perspectives on current political controversies from a non-European perspective.

With the exception of this HSU, the WG's final proposals are vulnerable to the charge of ethnocentrism, both because of the version of world history promoted and also because they ignore the fact that the UK is a multicultural society:

> It is unacceptable in multicultural Britain today, that primary children are insulated from the fact that Britain has been a nation of invaders, explorers, conquerors and slave owners. The foundations of the Empire rested on such

activities. Only in this context can the unit on exploration and encounters have any meaning and relevance to British history. It is difficult to see how the working group could have omitted the famous ships – the slavers – from the exemplary information on ships and seafarers. (Fisher, 1990, p. A18)

Fisher goes on to assert that the omission of the whole history of the slave trade from the proposed History curriculum is an example of 'mental colonisation'. Although by failing to mention HSU 38 his views could be seen to lack balance, he is right to insist that this distorted view of world history will only help to perpetuate distorted and racist views within British society. This possibility was only enhanced by Secretary of State MacGregor's revisions to the WG's Final Report.

Religious Education is part of the National Curriculum, though since it is not to be assessed its status is different from other subjects. There will be no working group to establish a national RE curriculum. However, the 1988 Act itself laid down clear guidelines for both the daily acts of collective worship and for the RE curriculum. For the RE curriculum 'Any agreed syllabus ... shall reflect the fact that the religious traditions in Great Britain are in the main Christian whilst taking account of the teaching and practices of the other principal religions represented in Britain' (*The Education Reform Act 1988*, p. 6). There is more freedom and flexibility here than for the collective worship which 'shall be wholly or mainly of a broadly Christian character' (*The Education Reform Act 1988*, p. 5). Every encouragement needs to be given to the Standing Advisory Councils on Religious Education (SACREs), to schools and to teachers, and perhaps ultimately to courts and to judges to interpret these terms of legislation as liberally and tolerantly as possible. It remains the case that these clauses are, and were intended to be, a direct attack on education for a multicultural society. The Act puts teachers and schools in the position of having to propagate and extol one of the religions of the UK against the others. This is to use the state school system in the service of religious intolerance. It is to bring the state into religious disputes in a way that has scarcely happened since Catholic emancipation. It is more than another example of neo-assimilationism; it subjects non-Christian children to practices and teaching which may well be profoundly culturally offensive; it provides those white parents and children who may be racist with a ready stick with which to beat any headteacher or teacher whom they consider to be too multicultural.

There are, then, elements within the emerging National Curriculum which are nationalist and/or racist. In case the contradictions and conflicts here are not obvious they can be briefly enumerated. Firstly, and most importantly, the nationalist curriculum is in conflict with large sections of the population of England and Wales. If the compulsory and state-endorsed curriculum finds no room for various groups' literary products, ignores or travesties the part they have played in the history of the world, of Europe and of the UK, relegates their languages to the second division where they need never be a matter of any interest to any white child, and subjects their children to the practices of an alien religion, then these groups will experience schools as increasingly hostile places. If those white pupils and parents who are racist are allowed to celebrate English triumphalist history or literature or to use the terms of the Act itself to minimize the cultural acknowledgement of other groups in the daily life of the school, then educational institutions are playing a part in raising and exacerbating racial and group conflicts instead of reducing and resolving them. Secondly, there is a conflict with the UK's membership of the EC. To the extent to which the History proposals miss the opportunity for stressing cross-European influences and movements, they amplify that uncertainty towards the emergent European state which is a feature of current government policy. Thirdly, there is a conflict with the UK's aspiration to remain a significant force in world trade. By limiting the nation's language skills to those of the EC and by not maximizing the advantages which could be derived from its multilingual population, and by the encouragement of ethnocentrism and insularity, the National Curriculum fails to encourage the attitudes and skills needed successfully to develop the UK's economic and political role beyond the EC.

THE NATIONAL CURRICULUM: THEORY AND PRACTICE

By 1990 the implementation of the National Curriculum was suffering from a credibility gap in schools, especially in primary schools. This was partly due to overkill: the amount of paper coming from the NCC, the DES, the LEAs and SEAC had become impossible to read, let alone internalize and contextualize against every other piece of paper. In primary schools where heads and teachers needed to read all the material, not just those of a secondary subject specialism, the burden had reached hysterical proportions. At the same time reports were coming in that the piloting of the first round of Standard Assessment Tasks (SATs) had been little short of a disaster (see Chapter 3). There were, however, more fundamental and enduring reasons for concern over the implementation.

The difficulty of the subject discipline approach was becoming more apparent at primary level. The Working Group approach of subject experts each greedy for timetable time not only reinforced this impression but established the apparently endless sequence of papers, each placing particularistic demands on schools and each ultimately backed by statute. The trap of the ten levels of attainment (discussed in Chapter 3) and of proliferating ATs was increasingly evident.

In secondary schools there were worries about the way in which assessment at key stage 4 was likely to affect the only recently established GCSE exams. The tensions between the need for specialisms and the wide subject based curriculum enforced by the 1988 Act were becoming particularly visible for the 14 to 16 age group. Indeed, Secretary of State MacGregor had at last acknowledged that the curriculum for this phase needed radical rethinking. At the same time the outdated nature of much of the sixth form curriculum was increasingly being exposed, but with little hope of reform while the concentration of the DES, the LEAs and schools was on the compulsory curriculum phase.

Those concerned with the teaching of special needs were also raising anxieties, not only about the effect of the implementation of the 1988 Act in general but also about the National Curriculum in particular. Each glossy brochure from the NCC and the DES contained at least one paragraph to the effect that the National Curriculum is for all children. But those responsible for teaching the profoundly handicapped, as well as those working with children and young people whose self-confidence had been badly damaged by failure in school, were less optimistic about the facile claims to entitlement. Reading the proliferating lists of attainment targets, they acknowledged that for some of their pupils they were pure irrelevance, and that for others they offered little beyond repeated public failure. The National Curriculum seemed to be asserting that handicap could be cured by insisting that all children learn the same material. Whilst many special needs teachers aspired towards full curricular integration for the maximum number of children, they acknowledged, as the NCC apparently did not, that for some children this could be at best a forlorn hope, at worst a humiliating infliction.

In all areas of schooling it was being recognized that teachers were being asked to make bricks without straw. An already underfunded public service was being asked to take on the major National Curriculum initiative without any additional resources. In terms of technological equipment and teaching materials alone the additional demands on school resources were considerable. Perhaps even more important was the size of the in-service education of teachers (INSET) job which needed to be done, especially in primary schools. Heads were becoming aware of this INSET need at the same time that they were having to develop entirely new skills themselves in terms of the local management of schools (see Chapter 5). In the area of special educational needs the aspirations of the National Curriculum were seen to be increasingly unrealizable within the current funding conditions and arrangements. Indeed, the Education, Science and Arts Committee of the House of Commons, which is bipartisan, noted that without appropriate extra support and provision the National Curriculum could not successfully be taught to many children with special educational needs. The Committee pointed out that the 1988 Act is likely to endanger that aspiration towards the education of children perceived to have special needs in mainstream schools which was the main thrust of the 1981 Act:

> some of the effects of the 1988 Education Reform Act on the 1981 Education Act are as yet uncertain and not recognised. The Department's policy on special needs should be developed in conjunction with its policies on LMS and the National Curriculum and not in isolation from them, as it appears to be. There is no guarantee under the 1988 Act that children with the wider range of special educational needs in mainstream schools will receive the support and extra provision they require to gain access to the National Curriculum. Neither is there any guarantee that the process

of integration supported by the 1981 Education Act will be able to continue under LMS. (Education, Science and Arts Committee, 1990, pp. vii–viii)

The Committee here notes one of the contradictions between the terms of the 1988 Act in emphasizing that the local management of schools is likely to result in formulae for resourcing which do not sufficiently acknowledge the provision for special educational needs. Far from gaining the right to an entitlement curriculum, it will become more difficult for mainstream schools to continue the trend towards the integration of children with special needs.

The government had established a further major contradiction between the legislation it wished to implement and those chosen to do the implementing – a poorly paid, demoralized teaching force, working in under-resourced schools and increasingly uncertain about both the viability and the desirability of the initiative. The possibility of conflict was emerging at school level between what teachers were told to do by the NCC and SEAC and what they saw as practicable and in the best educational interests of their pupils. At a headteachers' conference in the summer of 1990 a head was cheered when she announced that she would break the law rather than repeat the National Curriculum standardized testing exercise in her school. As headteachers steered warily around the legislation on collective acts of worship and wondered how they could ever implement the National Curriculum Technology without the necessary equipment or teacher expertise, conflict over the National Curriculum and testing had become an element of daily school life.

REFERENCES

- Bash, L., Coulby, D. and Jones, C. (1985) *Urban Schooling: Theory and Practice*. London: Cassell.
- Bash, L. and Coulby, D. (1989) *The Education Reform Act: Competition and Control*. London: Cassell.
- Bibby, B. (1990) Why final orders create a multicultural gap. *Times Educational Supplement*, 29 June, p. 23.
- Coulby, D. (1990) The construction and implementation of the primary core curriculum. In Coulby, D. and Ward, S. (eds) *The Primary Core National Curriculum: Policy into Practice*. London: Cassell.

• DES (1988) *Report of the Committee of Inquiry into the Teaching of English*. London: HMSO.
• DES (1989) *National Curriculum: From Policy to Practice*. London: DES.
• DES (1990) *History for Ages 5 to 16: Proposals of the Secretary of State for Education and Science*. London: DES.
• DES and Welsh Office (1988) *English for Ages 5 to 11*. London: DES and Welsh Office.
• DES and Welsh Office (1989a) *English for Ages 5 to 16*. London: HMSO.
• DES and Welsh Office (1989b) *English in the National Curriculum*. London: HMSO.
• Education, Science and Arts Committee (1990) *Staffing for Pupils with Special Educational Needs* (Fifth Report). London: HMSO.
• Fisher, G. (1990) An insulated island race. *Times Educational Supplement*, 11 May, p. A18.
• Freire, P. (1972) *Pedagogy of the Oppressed*. Harmondsworth: Penguin.
• Hickox, M. and Moore, R. (1990) TVEI, vocationalism and the crisis of liberal education. In Flude, M. and Hammer, M. (eds), *The Education Reform Act 1988: Its Origins and Implications*. London: Falmer.
• History Working Group (1989) *Interim Report*. London: DES and Welsh Office.
• History Working Group (1990) *Final Report*. London: DES and Welsh Office.
• Modern Foreign Languages Working Group (1990) *Initial Advice*. London: DES and Welsh Office.
• Nash, I. (1989) Cox 'threatened to resign'. *Times Educational Supplement*, 21 April, p. A1.
• Nash, I. (1990) Multicultural links cut from English report. *Times Educational Supplement*, 8 June, p. A1.
• Nash, I. and Darking, L. (1990) Thatcher's disapproval holds up history report. *Times Educational Supplement*, 30 March, p. 1.
• NCC (1989a) *English 5-11*. York: NCC.
• NCC (1989b) *Curriculum Guidance 1: A Framework for the Primary Curriculum*. York: NCC.
• NCC (1990) *Curriculum Guidance 3: The Whole Curriculum*. York: NCC.

• Rumbold, A. (1990) Correct English. *Times Educational Supplement*, 15 June, p. A17.

• St John-Brooks, C. (1990) Something has to give – but what? *Times Educational Supplement*, 21 September, p. 10.

• Task Group on Assessment and Testing (1987) *A Report*. London: DES.

• *The Education Reform Act 1988*. London: HMSO.

• *Times Educational Supplement* (1990) Cultural Tests. *Times Educational Supplement*, 8 June, p. A23.

• Ward, S. (1990) The core National Curriculum in an integrated context. In Coulby, D. and Ward, S. (eds) *The Primary Core National Curriculum: Policy into Practice*. London: Cassell.

• Wragg, T. (1988) *Education in the Market Place: The Ideology behind the 1988 Education Bill*. London: National Union of Teachers.

3
Assessment

David Coulby

ASSESSMENT AND THE 1988 EDUCATION ACT

The division between Chapters 2 and 3 in this book is purely a matter of organization. As the number of references common to this chapter and the previous one indicate, it is not really possible to discuss the National Curriculum separately from the associated assessment arrangements. Secretary of State MacGregor reminded teachers in 1990: 'Assessment is intrinsic to the National Curriculum' (MacGregor, 1990a, p. 12). In terms of the politics of social policy this could be stated even more emphatically: the National Curriculum has been introduced in order that there should be national testing.

The theme of internal contradiction is, in an important way, less helpful with regard to assessment. The assessment arrangements, on the contrary, may be seen as the hub around which many of the important components of the 1988 Act revolve. In particular, the assessment components of the legislation need to be understood alongside those on open enrolment and the local management of schools (LMS).

Sections 26–32 of the 1988 Act allows schools to recruit beyond their previously planned admission levels. Effectively, this means that if schools so wish they may increase the number of pupils they teach. The reason given for doing this is that it will expand parental choice. Prior to 1988, LEAs had been able to balance intakes to all the schools within a locality. To do this they needed, in some cases where schools were not recruiting sufficiently highly, to place children in schools which had not been their parents' first preference. This had meant that some parents were disappointed in their first choice of school (for an analysis of the way in which government policy on schools has, in part, been driven by the rising number of parents disappointed with the secondary school which the LEA has allocated to their child, see Stillman, 1990). By opening enrolment the 1988 Act allows parents to have more freedom of choice of primary and secondary schools. Schools might themselves not wish to expand the number of pupils they teach, but this is where another section of the Act comes into play.

Sections 33–51 of the Act establish the arrangements for LMS. Under these, large schools will achieve a considerable degree of financial autonomy (see Chapter 5) and, more important for the argument here, all schools will be funded by formula. These formulae vary between LEAs, though all must be DES approved. However, the most important component in all the formulae is student numbers; quite reasonably, the more pupils you have on roll, the more resources the school receives. The language of the day spelt this out in these graphic terms: 'think of each pupil as a sack of cash'. The application of the formulae to schools meant that in many cases there was considerable pressure on resources. So intense was this pressure that some schools found that they were unable to continue to employ the same number of teachers as previously. In these conditions they were understandably anxious to recruit as many pupils as possible, thereby to appropriate the accompanying sacks of cash and minimize resource cuts and staff redundancies. In this environment schools were not only happy to expand their numbers, they actively set about publicity campaigns and recruitment drives to further this end. The 1988 Act had succeeded in its aim of encouraging competition between schools – competition to obtain the maximum number of pupils.

With parents seen as the consumers of schools in an open market (see Bash and Coulby, 1989, Chapter 2), the assessment arrangements can be better understood. Prior to 1988 parental choice of school had not necessarily been well informed. The requirements of the 1980 and 1986 Acts for the publication of public exam results to all parents within a school had little effect on the parents of primary or lower secondary pupils. Even for those parents who understood the significance of these results, they could have no relevance for the selection of primary school. Parental choice was as often as not based on not very well founded and almost certainly out-of-date rumour, on which school had the uniform most closely approaching a 1920s stereotype or on performance in the locally favoured team sport. What the assessment arrangements provide is an apparently rational basis for the parental selection of schools. With all the results published for all the profile components of all the subjects of the National Curriculum at key stages 2–4 – and indeed, if schools follow the encouragement of the Secretary of State, at key stage 1 too – parents will be provided with clear league tables for each subject. (Key stage 1 is at age 7, key stage 2 at 11, key stage 3 at 14, and key stage 4 at 16.) Since these league tables come endorsed by the DES, they will appear to carry all the status of truth, and will provide the trusted basis for parental choice of school.

In terms of the political purposes of the 1988 Act, then, it is important to see how these three components – open enrolment, LMS and published test results – hang together. The assessment arrangements fulfil a further political purpose in that they will provide apparently objective measures of the relative success of schools. They may be taken alongside the quantity of resources available under formula to provide the kind of cost indicators of the relative effectiveness of schools which might be seen as helpful to, for instance, Treasury evaluations (see Coulby, 1989). Whatever might be their effect on the teaching and learning of pupils, the assessment arrangements, and in particular the requirements to publish results, will make schools more account-able both to parents and to those ultimately responsible for providing resources for state education. Prowse accurately comments: 'The testing machinery is intended not just to keep pupils' noses to the grindstone, but to exert discipline over teachers and schools' (Prowse, 1989).

One of the major uses of summative testing is to place pupils and students into some form of hierarchical order. Given that the workplaces to which these young people are destined are organized in ways which demand a high degree of both specialism and hierarchy, it is difficult to see how this could be otherwise. Examination and assessment systems perform this function of differentiating the workforce for the benefit of selection pro-cedures at the workplace. The issues discussed below concern con-tradictions and conflicts around how this testing should take place, at what age, how often and with what degree of publicity. Whether the actual developing needs of the contemporary economy are best met by a hierarchically structured workforce is a question which is not addressed. If such stratification does not meet the actual needs of the workplace then an even more fundamental contradiction may yet emerge.

CONFLICTS OVER THE IMPLEMENTATION OF THE ASSESSMENT ARRANGEMENTS

Whilst, in terms of policy formulation, this may be an area of government policy characterized by consistency rather than contradiction, its implementation has hardly been without conflict. Conflicts have revolved around how much could be assessed, who should be responsible for the assessment, how the assessing should actually be carried out in schools, how the ultimate results should be recorded, and how and to whom they should be published. These various issues are covered in this section.

Secretary of State Baker's warm welcome for the Task Group on Assessment and Testing Report (TGAT, 1987) was explained as being because it not only seemed to make his aims realizable but, further, to provide a testing framework less unacceptable to the profession than had earlier been anticipated (Bash and Coulby, 1989, Chapter 4). The acceptance of the TGAT proposals was, however, to lead to a good deal of conflict within the government itself since it subsequently transpired, via a leaked letter from her private office, that the then Prime Minister Margaret Thatcher was far from happy with the Group's recommendations. She recognized that these would lead to a costly testing apparatus; leave authority with teachers (even worse, 'She is also concerned to note the major role envisaged for LEAs in the implementation of the system' (*The Independent*, 10 March 1988, p. 1)); take a considerable amount of time to implement, and not provide the clear public yardstick of cost effectiveness for which she was looking. She did, by contrast, want short, sharp, cheap, nationally administered tests with clear league-table-style published results. By June 1988, when in a parliamentary written answer the Secretary of State was able to announce the government's adoption of many of the TGAT recommendations, it seemed as if he had won this particular battle. In terms of their administration, at least in primary schools, by LEAs, this remains the case. However, the conflict between the Baker (TGAT) and the Thatcher view of testing continued to pose major difficulties in implementation. The TGAT recommendations were in conflict with the political objectives of national testing – to control teachers and to encourage competition. This contradiction has proved a major difficulty for SEAC and for three Secretaries of State.

As each Working Group advocated impressive and comprehensive lists of Attainment Targets (ATs), the amount of material actually to be assessed rapidly built up (see *The Overcrowded Curriculum* in Chapter 2). Previous public exam practice in the UK had been to select questions from a large body of knowledge. This meant that pupils and students had to learn the whole of the area but that they were ultimately only tested on a small part of it. The TGAT recommendations (TGAT, 1987), based on the more comprehensive testing technique of graded assessment, make this form of sampling apparently impossible. There needs to be a statement of how far each pupil has progressed on each AT at each key stage. Perhaps members of the TGAT Committee did not foresee the proliferation of ATs. Certainly as each WG's report was published the TGAT proposals looked increasingly less workable. In addition to the difficulty of the ever-growing number of ATs, the TGAT methodology itself created the potential for a further nightmare of time-consuming testing bureaucracy. Since each AT within the TGAT framework was to be tested by a Teacher Assessment (TA) and by a Standard Assessment Task (SAT) and since there was then to be moderation both within school and between schools, the organization of national testing seemed to be in danger of taking over the school system completely.

It was against this background that in the spring of 1990 Secretary of State MacGregor made a critical announcement with regard to key stage 1. He said that, at this stage, children should only be assessed on the three foundation subjects:

> When it comes to assessing 7 and 11 year olds in technology, history and geography, I have announced that I have it in mind to simplify arrangements in order to ease the burden on primary school teachers. In the case of 7 year olds certainly, my provisional view is that it should *not* be a statutory requirement for schools to administer Standard Assessment Tasks when settling the end-of-key-stage statutory assessments in these subjects. Similar principles might also apply to the assessment of pupils at the age of 11 in these subjects. (MacGregor, 1990, pp. 15–16)

Given that Technology, History and Geography were at the top of the chronological pecking order of non-core foundation subjects, it is clear that this announcement may be taken to apply to all these subjects. Indeed, when subsequently the initial letters of guidance were issued to the WGs on Music, Art and PE, it was made clear to them right from the start that, far from coming out with an empire-building list of ATs, they were to accept that assessment in their subjects would be much less detailed than for the other foundation subjects. Thus, in the extreme case of PE:

> The Secretary of State intends that because of the nature of the subject, the objectives (attainment targets) and means of achieving them (programmes of study) should not be prescribed in as much detail for PE as for the core and other foundation subjects. He considers that schools and teachers should have substantial scope here to develop their own schemes of work. *It is the task of the PE Working Group to advise on a statutory framework which is sufficiently broad and flexible to allow schools wide discretion in relation to the matters to be studied.* (DES, 1990a)

Secretary of State MacGregor has thus abandoned the principle of compulsory national assessment in *all* National Curriculum foundation subjects at key stage 1 and has hinted that he intends to do the same for key stage 2.

Interestingly, what MacGregor has actually done is stick to the TGAT mode of assessment (that is, full coverage of all ATs along with the TA, SAT and moderation paraphernalia) at the cost of national assessment of the full primary curriculum. It appears that national tests of all subjects are less important than elaborately rigorous assessment of the three core areas. MacGregor made this decision before the issue of the format of the SATs was finalized. In doing this he perhaps attempted to pre-empt any intervention from his own party which might have demanded more traditional (and simpler and cheaper) modes of testing. He seems to have avoided Margaret Thatcher's preferred option at the expense of sacrificing his predecessor's aspiration to national assessment of all subjects for all compulsory school age pupils.

This shows some awareness of the practicalities of testing in primary schools, but it is a considerable climb-down. The climbdown is no less noticeable in that the assessment of non-core foundation subjects is to be left to the otherwise devalued Teacher Assessment (see pp. 46–7). Whether it is sufficient of a climbdown to bring the testing arrangements within realistic levels and to prevent a repetition of the disastrous piloting of the SATs in primary schools (see pp. 50–2) remains to be seen. Indeed, despite the restricted number of subjects to be given SATs, in the summer of 1990 the School Examinations and Assessment Council (SEAC) at last recommended that the ATs should be sampled by the testing arrangements and not comprehensively covered (Makins, 1990). When the SATs for key stage 1 in 1991 were ultimately revealed, they were indeed for a narrow selection of ATs in English, Maths and Science. Clarke had expediently forsaken both Baker's range of subjects and TGAT's comprehensive mode of assessment.

Given that the nature of the competitive pressures described in the section above means that teachers and headteachers are likely to prioritize those subjects which are assessed – and only those – in their planning and teaching, MacGregor's restriction on the subjects to the core alone could be taken to mean that six-ninths of the National Curriculum has effectively been abandoned at infant level and may soon be similarly discarded for the junior phase. If the core subjects only are to be nationally assessed, it is likely to be these which will be pre-eminently stressed in primary schools. Even so, the weight of the assessment task will be considerable. Gipps, taking a primary class of 30 children approaching their key stage 1 assessment in the three core subjects only, calculates:

> A simple calculation of the number of attainment targets, by the number of statements of attainment, by the levels, by the number of children in the class ($33 \times 3 \times 3 \times 30$) shows that there is a potential pool of 8,910 bits of information for a teacher of seven-year-olds to deal with. And then of course there will be CDT [*sic*], history and geography, and by age 11 any class could cover four or five levels of attainment, so the number of bits of information will increase. (Gipps, 1990, p. 96)

Even though Clarke has dramatically reduced the extent to which the SATs will check the ATs, the TA must still cover them all. As well as being understood all this information has to be recorded and much of it fed back to pupils and parents in as meaningful a manner as possible.

Moving to the issue of who should be responsible for the assessment, the conflict has revolved around whether the results of the Teacher Assessment (TA) or Standard Assessment Task (SAT) should ultimately be given credence. The TGAT Report had lulled teachers into a sense of false security (Coulby, 1989), not least by giving the impression that class teachers' own judgements would be at the centre of the National Curriculum testing arrangements. In the event this was not to be the case. SEAC recommended that the SATs should have priority (Halsey, 1989). It is interesting that press reports again suggested that Prime Ministerial interference lay behind the ultimate decision to take SEAC's advice rather than that of TGAT:

> Mrs Thatcher has over-ruled the advice of Government-appointed experts as well as that of her former Education Secretary, Mr Kenneth Baker, by insisting that children are rated according to nationally prescribed tests rather than by their teachers.... Mrs Thatcher's determination to downgrade teachers' views and force schools to rely more on banks of national tests now appears to have won the day. (Tester, 1989, p. 58)

Behind the moderating and appeals procedures which were finally implemented (DES, 1990b), the decision not to trust teachers' judgements is clearly revealed.

The way in which assessment should be carried out in schools became a particularly contentious issue when the first SATs, drawn up by the three consortia of LEAs, academic departments of education and commercial publishers, were piloted with infant children in the spring of 1990. There were reports of children in tears and teachers stressed to breaking point:

> Teachers unanimously described the SATs' workload as 'overwhelming'. One school reported teachers receiving 21 lbs of SATs material each.

> Teachers described how the pilot SATs had completely dominated the curriculum for the period of the trials.

> Teachers also reported deteriorating behaviour in pupils as a result of classes being so unsettled for the 5 weeks.

Teachers reported increased symptoms of stress, exhaustion in themselves and in their pupils, and felt reluctant to teach Year 2 pupils in future in view of the administrative demands of the SATs.

Some teachers have been sufficiently disillusioned by the process to contemplate resignation or early retirement. (National Union of Teachers, 1990, pp. 2–5)

One LEA, Sheffield, actually pulled out of the entire piloting exercise because of the upset that had been caused to pupils and teachers.

An education junior minister, Alan Howarth, admitted there had been difficulties. It is interesting to see how this was reported in the *Daily Mail*. Under the front page headline 'Betrayal of our children', Massey wrote:

The much-heralded school tests designed to assess Britain's seven-year-olds are totally inadequate ... Our investigations show that they fail in their aim of ensuring that youngsters have grasped fundamental reading, spelling and numeracy skills.

The tests have little to do with the basics of the three Rs. Instead, they concentrate on assessing a pupil's innate potential, with vague tasks and puzzles.... As the campaign for a sweeping review of the tests gained momentum, Education Minister Alan Howarth conceded last night that the Standard Assessment Tasks were unworkable in their present form.

'It seems from the early anecdotal evidence I have heard about the trials that those used this summer were too demanding of teachers and pupils and need to be slimmed down'. (Massey, 1990, p. 1)

If the *Daily Mail*, the National Union of Teachers and the DES were not happy with the SATs, it was difficult to imagine who was. But it was not these dissatisfactions, either from within his own party or elsewhere, that informed Secretary of State MacGregor when he eventually attempted to lift the testing burden on schools. As stated above he preferred to restrict the range of subjects to be tested rather than necessarily restrict the complex mode of assessment.

Whilst Massey was concerned about the three Rs, others were

noting the amount of time that the assessment and recording exercise was taking away from teaching and learning. The size of the testing enterprise was beginning to emerge along with the fact that the government had allowed itself to be steered by TGAT into uncharted waters: 'Ministers should note that no other country accepts the need for external tests of the complexity and frequency envisaged in the UK' (Prowse, 1989, p. 23). Clarke's restriction on the amount of SAT material to be used at key stage 1 in 1991 has clear implications for key stage 2 and beyond. Indeed, it was followed by the announcement that key stage 3 assessment should rely on short tests rather than emulate the elaborate key stage 1 SATs. It seems that, as a result of the impracticality of its earlier SAT proposals and trials, the government will be forced to rely on TAs. The SATs will be shorter and sharper; they will be given prominence over TAs. Despite her departure from Downing Street, Thatcher's views on testing have apparently prevailed.

The conflict over how the test results should be recorded is complex because it is intertwined with the dispute over records of achievement (for terminology in this area, see Ritchie, 1990). Records of achievement had been successfully developed and, with the help of a DES-resourced initiative, disseminated at secondary level. It had been expected that the work done in this area would lead to a national system of records of achievement. Further, by using records in the primary phase in the way developed by the ILEA Language Record (Barrs *et al.*, 1990) and advocated by the Language WG (DES and Welsh Office, 1989), it might have been possible to use records of achievement to present the assessment at the key stages within the context of an evolving and rounded profile of each pupil. Such a profile would have had the potential to involve both parents and pupils in the processes of assessing progress and setting objectives. SEAC reported favourably on both the introduction of a national system for secondary schools and on the expansion of records into the primary phase (SEAC, 1989). Yet when Angela Rumbold, as Minister of State for Education, responded to this report (Rumbold, 1989) she ignored the issue of records of achievement and chose only to comment on the statutory arrangements needed for reporting the results of the National Curriculum assessment. This caused much anger among those who had helped to develop the work on records: 'The Government's decision to turn its back entirely on records of achievement, except for the reporting of national curriculum attainment ... is not only breathtaking in its duplicity but is also flying in the face of the overwhelmingly positive response to the initiative from educationalists and employers' (Munby, 1989, p. 21).

Both the formal arrangements for recording national test results and the national scheme of records of achievement were finalized with the publication of DES Circular 8/90 (DES, 1990c). Although its title is *Records of Achievement*, this is misleading: what it actually outlines is a system of minimal recording of progress through the ATs. It does, however, leave schools and LEAs the opportunity to integrate these within a broader frame of records of achievement. Furthermore, it establishes a minimum framework which consistently incorporates both primary and secondary schools. It also encourages the establishment of substantial records of achievement schemes and commends the guidelines established by the doomed Training Agency (from whence perhaps came the pressure for this about-turn). In the end the decision whether to adopt the minimal legal records or to adopt substantial records of achievement will rest with LEAs and schools. The decision here is of major importance. Whilst some schools and LEAs may continue with records of achievement, the consistency and currency (especially with parents and employers) of a national scheme will still be lacking. However, records of achievement present schools with the possibility of making the assessment of the National Curriculum more than just a paper exercise. By maintaining a record owned by the child and regularly reviewed with both the pupil and her/his parents/carers, it may be possible to regain the notion of formative assessment so forcefully argued in the TGAT Report. Records of achievement could be the instrument whereby the external monolith of the National Curriculum is humanized to the needs and development of individual pupils. But when used in this way records of achievement are themselves exceedingly costly in terms of teacher time. It is more likely that back-to-basics recording will be what is needed to accompany back-to-basics testing.

The publication of results is closely related to the issue of records. Records of achievement are themselves a means by which a pupil's progress can be publicized, but in this case the audience is chosen by the pupil concerned who may also choose not to disclose the record to a particular audience. It is the publication of results which lies at the very heart of reservations about National Curriculum and testing. Teachers of all age levels assess children on a regular basis to establish what has been learned, how quickly they can move on to the next theme and where repetition or remedial action is necessary. Their assessments do not carry the weight of national legislation; their results are not always made known to the pupils concerned, let alone to their parents/carers, the headteacher, the LEA or the DES. Performed in this way, as the TGAT Report stressed (TGAT, 1987), assessment is simply an integral part of good teaching. It is the making public of the results of these tests, so that one way or another they are available not only to parents but to peers and the wider community of the school, that can result in the generation of competitiveness and the ascription of negative labels which are discussed in the final two sections of this chapter.

RESOURCING NATIONAL ASSESSMENT

Another main area where there is a contradiction between the testing arrangements and other areas of government policy is with regard to the likely cost of implementing the policy. The three consortia (mentioned above) of LEAs, higher education institutions and publishers, spent £6 million solely on the development and initial piloting of the SATs for key stage 1. By 1989 a total of £20 million had been spent simply on the development of SATs at key stages 1 and 3 (Nash, 1989, p. 4). SEAC's own corporate plan for 1990 envisaged its expenditure rising from almost £17.25 million per year in 1990/1 to nearly £26.5 million per year in 1992/3 (SEAC, 1990, p. 30). Some commentators' estimates have made these increases seem modest:

> Annual costs for the tests will swallow up more money than most schools currently spend in an entire year, exam experts in Essex predict, after an extensive in-service teacher-training programme which involved all teachers in its 750 primary and secondary schools. ... [If the Essex predictions are confirmed] then the global exam costs will rise by even more than the £100 million to £200 million predicted last month ... by Professor Desmond Nuttall. (Nash, 1989, p. 4)

The expenditure of resources on the establishment of a vast

testing bureaucracy needs to be contrasted with severe impoverishment elsewhere in the education service. At the same time as the testing bureaucracy was being established, many inner city schools were having major difficulties recruiting people to poorly-paid teaching jobs.

But the testing empire itself is only one component of the costs that will be involved in the implementation of the scheme of national testing. If the scheme is to have a chance of success it will need to be backed by major INSET initiatives. Whilst at secondary level these may be contained because teachers are working with subject-based material with which they are already exceedingly familiar, in primary schools the task will be much more formidable. Primary teachers are themselves without confidence that they have the expertise to teach the whole range of National Curriculum subjects. Assessing even the three core subjects is likely to prove a major challenge and in addition primary teachers are to be solely responsible for the assessment of the non-core subjects. They will only meet this challenge with confidence and the appropriate expertise if considerable time is spent familiarizing them with the materials and the processes. The costs of advisory teachers, training, staff release and supply cover are funded to the LEAs from the DES via the Local Education Authority Training Grant Scheme (LEATGS). However, LEATGS only funds 65 per cent of these costs and there are important curriculum areas which it does not cover at all. The INSET duty will prove a major burden to LEAs, many of whom are struggling with budgets already inadequate due to the effect of poll tax–capping. Yet it was insufficient or non-existent INSET – admittedly assisted by unrealistic objectives and rank bad planning – which led to the fiasco of the SAT piloting exercise.

It is the LEAs which are to be given responsibility for the implementation of the testing arrangements at the primary phase, though probably not at the secondary (MacGregor, 1990b). In a statement which accompanied this announcement Secretary of State MacGregor said:

> LEAs and schools will need to make appropriate provision within the resources available to them for the establishment of these arrangements as an integral part of the National Curriculum. This will entail a redirection of the work of

LEAs, particularly their inspectors and advisers, as well as of schools. (DES, 1990d, p. 1)

It is clear from this statement that LEAs are being asked to take on a massive new role without any additional allocation of resources. Their responses to the announcement made it clear that they considered this to be impossible (Nash, 1990, p. 4).

Apart from the contradiction between introducing major new social policy initiatives without providing the resources to make them work, the announcement contains another potential source of conflict. LEA inspectors and advisers are unlikely to welcome the new role envisaged for them by the Secretary of State. Their own perception of their job is more likely to be to do with assisting heads and teachers in the implementation of curriculum and management of change than in terms of being the monitors for a lot of questionable tests which are to be handed down from the DES and SEAC. The announcement further underlines the precarious role of LEAs and their officers under the terms of the 1988 Act (see Chapter 1). Whether the people currently employed in these posts wish to take on the envisaged prefectorial role remains to be seen, but the DES may turn out not to have selected the most compliant task force for this purpose. Perhaps by placing LEAs and their officers in this ambiguous position central government is testing their future viability.

TEACHING, LEARNING AND ASSESSMENT

It is suggested at the opening of this chapter that the testing arrangements are what necessitate a National Curriculum rather than the other way around. One of the factors which substantiates this assertion is the amount of time that will be required of teachers for them to comply with the testing and recording regulations. There is a contradiction in this sense between the implementation of the National Curriculum in itself and the implementation of its associated assessment arrangements. As was described in Chapter 2, the National Curriculum is already overcrowded and there are real difficulties about squeezing it all into the time allocated for schooling. The assessment and recording arrangements will actually encroach upon valuable teaching time. Perhaps the architect of the Act did not trust teachers and headteachers to implement the National Curriculum without the tight regulations on assessment and public reporting. The priority given to the large amounts of time needed for assessing and recording at the expense of teaching and learning is an indication that it is the assessment of the National Curriculum rather than its specific content which is ultimately of the greater political importance.

The results in the National Curriculum tests are likely to be highly important to parents and to their children. For this reason, as well as for their statutory status, it is clear that teachers will do their best to ensure that all their pupils score as well as possible. This, in turn, is likely to influence the way in which teaching and learning is conducted in primary and secondary schools. Firstly, teachers are likely to give the highest priority to those subjects which are formally assessed. This means that those components of the school curriculum which are not part of the National Curriculum are increasingly likely to be marginalized and ignored. In primary schools, where it is the three core subjects (English, Mathematics, Science) which are to receive the overwhelming amount of formal, national assessment, even the other foundation subjects (Technology, History, Geography, Music, Art, PE) will have to fight hard to survive.

A second effect of the high status of the national test results may be teaching to the test, where teachers actually focus their lessons on the answers that will be required in the assessments. This may result in improved performances over time in the test results. However, as Gipps asks, 'if test results rise as a consequence of teaching to the test rather than as a consequence of some other change in the classroom process, is such a rise necessarily worth while?' (Gipps, 1990, p. 33).

The school curriculum and the National Curriculum are both likely to be affected by curriculum backwash where teachers concentrate their efforts only on that part of the curriculum which is going to be tested. Again, this can lead to the impoverishment of the curriculum in terms of its breadth. The themes, dimensions and skills which the National Curriculum Council (NCC) proclaim themselves as anxious to promote (see Chapter 2) are unlikely to receive much attention as the pressure of the importance of the test results makes itself felt on teachers and their curriculum planning.

Thirdly, there is serious contradiction between the overcrowded National Curriculum with the further loading that NCC

wish to give to it and the time-consuming assessment arrangements which will put pressure on teachers increasingly to restrict
their curriculum to the clear requirements of the tests. To the
extent to which there is conflict between the National Curriculum
and assessment, it is likely that the assessment will come to be
the pre-eminent force. Neither the blandishments of the NCC nor
their own sense of what constitutes a broad and balanced curriculum will be able to help teachers to withstand the pressure
from pupils, parents, headteachers, and indeed themselves, for
pupils to do as well as possible in the national tests.

ASSESSMENT AND COMPETITION

As indicated earlier in this chapter, it is the publication of
national test results which is one of the key mechanisms both in
ensuring the implementation of the National Curriculum and in
bringing about the wider aims of the 1988 Education Act. Among
these aims is the encouragement of competition at many different
levels (Bash and Coulby, 1989). This chapter concludes with an
examination of some of the likely effects of this competition.
It concentrates firstly on competition between pupils and then
on competition between schools.

The positive view about competition is that it serves to make
everyone perform better in the hope that they may win whatever
glittering prizes are on offer. What is often not given so much
attention among the plaudits awarded to the winners is what happens to those who lose. Since the issue here concerns children – in
the case of key stage 1, very young children – care does need to
be paid to the consequences of failure for each individual child.
There will be hurt and disappointment on the part of parents and
probably of the child. There will be comparative conversations
between parents and between pupils. The results of these conversations may well be some name-calling in class or in the playground. There will be that modification of the view of the self
which ultimately leads so many young people to see themselves
as failures because their schools have failed them.

The process of labelling at school will begin early and will
carry the weight of national test results. The results of labelling in schools were previously taken very seriously (Hargreaves
et al., 1975) but it seems necessary, in the current climate, to
re-emphasize them. As far as teachers and parents are concerned

a label of low academic achievement can result in lowered expectations. These in turn can result in a reduction in the curriculum made available to a particular child in terms of both amount and level. Opportunities to stretch the child academically are less likely to be sought either at school or at home. The danger of the *state-endorsed label* which will be tagged to children early by the national testing is that it will be that much more difficult for the pupils themselves to resist. Their own expectation of themselves will be reduced; they will be unlikely to try so hard with school work; they may seek out a peer group of other children who seem not to be succeeding in order to minimize the competition, pressure and sense of failure. The effect of labelling children as failures is all too often to confirm the label by the effect that it has on people's subsequent expectations and behaviour. Whilst it is possible that competition in the national tests may raise standards for some children (Gipps, 1990, pp. 34–6), there is a strong likelihood that for others it will lower both standards and life chances.

Those who do least well in terms of academic achievement in schools come from particular groups in society. They are disproportionately from black and white working-class groups (Mortimore and Blackstone, 1982). If children from these groups are to succeed they need a school environment in which their contributions can be valued and in which they are given time to develop to their full potential in a positive and rewarding atmosphere. It has already been shown in the section on 'the nationalist curriculum' in Chapter 2 that certain non-white groups might well consider themselves ignored or even denigrated by the contents of the National Curriculum. White working-class children and young people might also find the reborn grammar school curriculum to be as alienating and irrelevant as its previous incarnation. The national tests will interpret this mismatch between the National Curriculum and large groups of children and young people only as failure by individual pupils. The national testing arrangements are likely to confirm and reinforce failure among those groups which have for so long been failed by schools.

The institutionalization of the process of labelling is often through streaming. The pressure on teachers and headteachers to deliver high scores in the national tests means that they are all the more likely to adopt the streaming strategy so that they can target groups for particular ATs. As well as being likely to restrict the possibilities of social integration in school for all children, for those in the lower streams this system only exacerbates the difficulties of low self- and teacher- expectations, restricted peer group interaction and reduced curricular opportunities. Another strategy likely to emerge is that of class groups based on levels of attainment rather than chronological age. The DES and the NCC are being cautious about the introduction of this possibility, but it is certainly an option they are attempting to propagate:

> There may be occasions in which individual children, clearly working well beyond the range of abilities in a class, may be helped by working with older children. DES Circular 6/89 states, however, that 'there is no expectation or requirement that pupils should be held back or pushed forward, except where the school judges this to be in the best interests of a pupil'. (NCC, 1989, p. 11)

This may well make teaching, and indeed assessment, more streamlined but it will bring to the schools of England and Wales a phenomenon not seen for many years – that of the older child, visibly noticeable, kept down with a younger peer group for one, two, or even three years.

Competition between schools will be, as explained in the first section of this chapter, for pupil numbers. It will increasingly be conducted on the basis of the results which pupils in the schools achieve in the national tests and the way in which these are presented to parents and the local press. It may be wise to be slightly cautious in making assumptions about the likely effects of this. According to Gipps, the parallel case of reporting secondary exam results has not made a major impact: 'Parents have had another piece of information on which to base their choice of school, but schools have not become obviously more "efficient", nor has there been widespread closing down of schools with exam results that are perceived to be poor' (Gipps, 1990, p. 42). There are, however, major differences between the national tests and secondary public exams. Firstly, the national tests will be taken by virtually all children. Secondly, they are available for four age stages beginning very early in the primary phase. Thirdly, because the terminology of the levels is going to be current right across the period of compulsory schooling, it will become much more widely understood than public examination grades. It is likely, then, that the national test results will inform parents' choice of school prior to starting primary school and at the stage of secondary transfer. It is further likely that some parents may decide to change their children's schools whilst they are actually within a particular phase, again on the basis of comparative test results.

Schools with disproportionately high numbers of white and black working-class children are less likely to be able to demonstrate successful national test results than those with predominantly middle-class children. Inner city schools and those in less privileged suburban housing areas will struggle to keep up with the results of the schools in the more leafy suburbs. The shift to formula funding will make this struggle all the harder, since the formulae are based mainly on absolute student numbers and can take little account of the particular needs of inner city schools which derive from the nature of their pupil intake. Of course schools will be able to publish a statement alongside their national test results explaining whether there are any special factors which affect them. In practice it is difficult to see how this will help. If some comparatively poor results are accompanied by a statement which says that the school has predominantly working-class children as pupils and that this explains the low achievement, it is difficult to see how either middle-class or working-class parents will be attracted to enrol their children. Similarly, explanations in terms of the numbers of bilingual pupils, children with special needs or one-parent families are likely to prove unattractive to all the potential clients of the school.

As the competition between schools increases, more attention and resources will need to be devoted to public relations. Many heads already consider their relations with the local press to be a major priority. Local newspapers are beginning to explore the opportunities for advertising from schools anxious to gain an edge in the market. The small devolved budgets of schools may well be squeezed by this extra demand upon them, which can only take resources away from teaching and learning. Other forms of seeking visibility within the community are also increasingly being pursued: the presentation of school uniforms and social events; the use of local community foci – doctors' surgeries, building society windows – as places to display children's work and other school achievements. The energy and resources which are increasingly being devoted to public relations are, in the main, taking senior staff time and scarce school resources away from the day-to-day teaching of the National Curriculum. Again the politics of the publication of results is in contradiction with the effective teaching of the subject matter of the National Curriculum.

Despite these efforts it is likely that some schools will lose children on the basis of parental choice informed by the national test results. It is not so much school closure that is the danger here. It is the instability in the system, generated firstly by the competition itself and secondly by the unplanned fluctuations in school rolls. The parents likely to shift their children to schools outside the local area are those with the access to and understanding of the published results and the national tests. They are those with the time and the transport available to deal with the complicated arrangements involved in taking a child several miles to school. They are likely to be predominantly middle class. The scenario which could develop is the rebirth of the slum school. An inner-city or predominantly working-class school does comparatively poorly on the published test results. Middle-class parents begin to transfer or admit their children to neighbouring schools. As a result the school in question receives less resources. With less resources and fewer high-achieving pupils the published results deteriorate even further. Soon the only pupils left are those whose parents do not have the knowledge, the commitment, or (most likely) the money, to shift them to another school. The danger is not that the school closes but that it remains open, a clearly underfunded third-class option for those who cannot send their children anywhere else.

If this were to be the case, the wider social contradictions suggested in Chapter 1 would have become evident. The 1988 Act may serve to heighten social division and conflict. One of the consequences of competition is greater and more visible difference between winners and losers. What the consequences of this widening division in educational and social terms will be remain to be seen. It is at least clear that the formulation and implementation of the legislation on the National Curriculum and assessment is a major lost opportunity. As an exercise in bringing competition and control into educational institutions, the initiative has done nothing to raise the educational achievement of the majority of pupils nor to increase the pool of skilled people available to potential employers. To the extent that the National Curriculum exercise will not, through the deleterious effects of the associated assessment arrangements, impede educational achievement for many children, it will provide only a time-wasting distraction for those genuinely engaged in attempting to improve the educational and life chances of the mass of children and young people.

REFERENCES

• Barrs, M. Ellis, S., Hester, H. and Thomas, A. (1990) *Patterns of Learning: The Primary Language Record and the National Curriculum.* London: Centre for Language in Primary Education.
• Bash, L. and Coulby, D. (1989) *The Education Reform Act: Competition and Control.* London: Cassell.
• Coulby, D. (1989) The hidden purpose behind testing. *The Independent,* 7 December.
• DES (1990a) Working Group on Physical Education: Terms of Reference, accompanying *The Department of Education and Science News: John MacGregor Announces Physical Education Working Group,* 231/90. London: DES.
• DES (1990b) *National Curriculum Assessment Arrangements. The Education (National Curriculum) Assessment Arrangements for English, Mathematics, and Science Order 1990.* London: DES.
• DES (1990c) *Circular 8/90: Records of Achievement.* London: DES.
• DES (1990d) *DES News 79/90: MacGregor Outlines National Curriculum Assessment Arrangements.* London: DES.
• DES and Welsh Office (1989) *English in the National Curriculum.* London: HMSO.
• Gipps, C. (1990) *Assessment: A Teachers' Guide to the Issues.* London: Hodder and Stoughton.
• Halsey, P. (1989) Letter to Secretary of State Baker on 'National Curriculum Assessment and Testing', 13 July. SEAC: London.
• Hargreaves, D., Hester, S. K. and Mellor, F. J. (1975) *Deviance in Classrooms.* London: Routledge and Kegan Paul.
• MacGregor, J. (1990a) *National Curriculum and Assessment: A Summary of Messages from Recent Speeches by the Rt. Hon. John MacGregor OBE MP, Secretary of State for Education and Science.* London: DES.

- MacGregor, J. (1990b) Letter to Philip Halsey, 'National Curriculum: Assessment arrangements for the core subjects at key stage 1', accompanying *DES News 79/90: MacGregor Outlines National Curriculum Arrangements*. London: DES.
- Makins, V. (1990) Slim down tests at 7, Minister told. *Times Educational Supplement*, 20 July, p. 2.
- Massey, R. (1990) Betrayal of our children. *Daily Mail*, 30 June, p. 1.
- Mortimore, J. and Blackstone, T. (1982) *Disadvantage and Education*. London: Heinemann.
- Munby, S. (1989) The month records died. *Times Educational Supplement*, 29 September, p. 21.
- Nash, I. (1989) Critics question costs of tests. *Times Educational Supplement*, 8 December, p. 4.
- Nash, I. (1990) LEAs to take charge of first curriculum tests. *Times Educational Supplement*, 9 March.
- National Union of Teachers (1990) *Testing: Who Carries the Load?* London: NUT.
- NCC (1989) *Curriculum Guidance 1: A Framework for the Primary Curriculum*. York: NCC.
- Prowse, M. (1989) A testing time for children. *Financial Times*, 26 October, p. 23.
- Ritchie, R. (ed.) (1990) *Profiling in Primary Schools*. Bath: Bath College of Higher Education.
- Rumbold, A. (1989) Letter to Philip Halsey, accompanying *Reporting Pupil Achievement Under the National Curriculum. (DES News 265/89)*. London: DES.
- SEAC (1989) *Records of Achievement: Report of Public Consultation*. London: SEAC.
- SEAC (1990) *The School Examinations and Assessment Council Corporate Plan 1990–93*. London: SEAC.
- Stillman, A. (1990) Legislating for Choice. In Flude, M. and Hammer, M. (eds) *The Education Reform Act 1988: Its Origins and Implications*. London: Falmer.
- Task Group on Assessment and Testing (1987) *A Report*. London: DES.
- Tester, N. (1989) Thatcher forces teachers out of curriculum test role. *Observer Education*, 22 October, p. 58.

4
The Progress of Restructuring

Geoff Whitty and Ian Menter

Many of the provisions in the Education Reform Act were intended to enhance parental choice and make schools more responsive to market forces. Open enrolment, local management of schools (LMS), grant-maintained schools (GMSs), city technology colleges (CTCs) can all be seen partly in this light. In reducing the powers of local education authorities (LEAs) to engage in the detailed planning of provision, they have also been seen as opening the way for a restructuring of the system as a whole. In particular, many people have predicted, notwithstanding the introduction of the National Curriculum, that the changes will lead to greater differentiation between schools (Bristol Polytechnic Education Study Group, 1989). While it may be an exaggeration to suggest that 'the main configurations of formal schooling will be unrecognizable by the mid-1990s' (Johnson, 1989), some significant changes in patterns of schooling are already beginning to emerge.

OPEN ENROLMENT

The Reform Act effectively removed 'artificial limits . . . on the ability of popular schools to recruit up to their available capacity' (DES, 1987a). The abolition of the right of LEAs to set Planned Admission Levels (PALs) up to 20 per cent below a school's 'standard number' (or even lower with DES approval) means that most schools may now recruit up to the level of their enrolments in 1979/80. It is claimed that the Act will increase the chances that pupils previously denied access to the most popular schools will now be able to attend them. But, beyond these individual benefits, one of the ideas behind open enrolment was that it would lead to systemic benefits by forcing the less popular schools to improve or, alternatively, to close.

65

Open enrolment has already been introduced for secondary schools and is soon to be extended to primary schools. A full assessment of its effects, and particularly its supposed effectiveness in disciplining poor schools, must await the implementation of LMS (see pp. 68–71), which ties funding directly to pupil numbers. There are, however, some initial causes for concern about its impact on comprehensive education. Some of these arise from the fact that the way in which the Act actually operates represents an uneasy compromise between the arguments of the free marketeers and those with more traditional conceptions of educational planning. Pressure from the former to allow popular schools to expand without limits was resisted. Furthermore, few LEAs have entirely abandoned their traditional procedures and priorities, particularly for 11+ transfer. In admissions to primary schools the same criteria are being used as previously, although there are indications that more parents than before are appealing against their allocation. In practice, some parents continue to be denied their choice and others experience no real widening of it.

Even though overall enrolments in most LEAs are now well below the 1979 level, the fact that popular schools cannot entirely meet demand allows some other schools to remain open despite a drop in popularity. Although some schools have become literally 'full', while others have fallen well below their old PALs, let alone their standard numbers, the latter will not necessarily become unviable. Meanwhile the popular schools, denied the opportunity to respond to their popularity by expansion beyond their standard number, are faced with the temptation of becoming covertly selective. Such selection would be likely to lead to the boosting of assessment test scores, which would give a misleading impression of the school's effectiveness and thus enhance its market appeal.

A little mentioned side-effect of this is that children moving into an area after annual allocation procedures have been completed are effectively denied choice of the better schools and their chances of an appeal succeeding are lower than under the old system where PALs left schools with considerable room for manoeuvre. The supposed advantages which the National Curriculum offers to children who move homes during their school careers are thus undermined by the ways in which the open enrolment clauses have been operated in some LEAs.

Another cause of concern is that the Labour Party's fear that 'these proposals will lead to educational apartheid and racially segregated schools' (quoted in Weekes, 1987) shows some signs of being realized. This concern arose partly from experience of the 'Dewsbury Affair', where white parents had sought to enrol their children in a primary school with fewer Asian pupils than the one to which they had been allocated. It was alleged that the Reform Bill was a charter for racist parents, but (while denying that segregation was any part of the Bill) the government argued that they did not wish 'to circumscribe [parental] choice in any way' (Blackburne, 1988). The implications of this became clear when, in April 1990, the Secretary of State seemed to take the view that a parent's right to choose a school overrides the 1976 Race Relations Act. The Commission for Racial Equality (CRE) had come to the conclusion that Cleveland County Council had acted unlawfully in allowing a child to transfer school on racial grounds. Although a subsequent decision by the parent to move the child again left the issue in limbo, the Secretary of State had already told the CRE that he planned to accept Cleveland's decision to permit the original transfer on the grounds that, if a school had spare places, parents did not have to give any reason for their preference. A spokesperson for the CRE was quoted as saying that the Secretary of State's claim 'is potentially a racist's charter. It could open the floodgates to every parent who objects to black children' (Hugill, 1990).

Not only has open enrolment restricted the power of LEAs to limit admissions to its schools, it has also potentially eroded the significance of LEA boundaries and the power of LEAs to plan provision on the basis of the needs of their own poll tax payers. The new Greenwich LEA sought to give priority to its own residents in allocating pupils to over-subscribed schools from September 1990. This was declared illegal after the authority had been taken to court by parents in neighbouring Lewisham (see Chapter 6 for other implications of this ruling). Although the grounds for the ruling were complicated by the fact that such parents had traditionally had the same rights as Greenwich residents under the ILEA, one of the Appeal Court judges argued that the criteria for admission to schools should be the same for all pupils irrespective of where they lived (Spencer, 1989). In other words political boundaries were, in principle, irrelevant in the context of parental choice. This had led some other authorities to review their allocation procedures.

LOCAL MANAGEMENT OF SCHOOLS

LMS was a reform that was welcomed in principle more widely than most of the other structural reforms. In practice, there was widespread opposition to the government's specific proposals (Ward, 1989). The overwhelming emphasis on age-weighted pupil numbers as the main basis for calculating budgets, and the government's lack of enthusiasm for complicated special needs formulae, represented a shift away from patterns of school resourcing that reflected the perceived level of need in a particular school as well as its size. A further major cause of consternation in many areas was the decision that most schools' budgets would have to be calculated on average teachers' salaries rather than the actual salaries of the teachers in particular schools. This meant that schools with a high proportion of teachers well up on the salary scales would find it difficult to manage within their allocated budgets.

Although most of the schemes of delegation devised by LEAs were accepted by the DES after minor modification, a few (including that of the once 'model' Tory authority, Croydon) were rejected and the LEAs concerned given an additional year to produce acceptable formulae. Most schemes of delegation, with the exception of those for inner London, began to come into effect on 1 April 1990. Even in the same area, different schools are at different stages of development in exploring the possibilities and problems with which LMS confronts them. Some schools have barely changed their mode of operation, whilst others have already introduced significantly new approaches to management and marketing. The attraction of experienced private sector managers onto school governing bodies, something which the government has sought to encourage through the 1986 Education Act, has proved easier for some schools than others and this has influenced the speed with which they have been able to respond to the demands of the Reform Act. There is some evidence that insufficient preparation for LMS has taken place in some areas and that governors are often far from clear about their new responsibilities. Nevertheless, the government believes that certain LEAs could have devolved more funding out of central administration and that some LEA staff are seeking to retain powers over individual schools that are inappropriate in the context of LMS (TES, 1990a). It has therefore decided to place new restrictions on the proportion of the overall budget that can be held back from schools.

The direct effects of LMS at school level are only just beginning to be seen, except in those areas that initiated the approach prior to the national legislation. Its full effects on the system as a whole will only gradually become clear as transitional arrangements are phased out. Knight (1990) suggests that, in time, LMS will produce greater differentiation between schools. If this follows the pattern of site-based management schemes in some parts of the USA, it could also produce a greater divergence in quality. Ball and Bowe (1990), in a detailed study of the effects of LMS in one comprehensive school in outer London, demonstrate some clear changes in the school's approach to decision-making but, disturbingly, they identify a tendency towards 'cost based decision making' at the expense of 'debates about the principles of educational provision'.

The relationship between school budgets generated by LMS formulae and the historic budgets of schools varies considerably across the country and within LEAs (Levacic, 1990). Overall, primary schools have tended to gain, while, in a number of LEAs, small secondary schools have lost out. There have also been some particular difficulties in LEAs containing highly contrasting catchment areas. In some of those LEAs, the effect of the formulae has been to move resources away from inner city schools or at least to give disproportionate benefits to suburban and rural schools.

Indeed, the effects of LMS formulae on inner city schools have been a cause of considerable disquiet. (This is further discussed in Chapter 5). The emphasis on pupil numbers is leading to the phasing-out of even the marginal attempts at positive discrimination that had developed since the 1960s. The initial attempt by the DES to discourage the introduction of additional factors to allow for social need or complicated formulae for identifying special educational needs has made LEAs reluctant to experiment with new forms of positive discrimination. In addition, many LEAs 'seem unclear as to whether special educational needs and social disadvantage are more or less the same thing or different issues' (Lee, 1990).

Other elements of the government's approach to LMS are

likely to have particular effects on inner city schools. The controversial decision to charge actual staffing costs against a budget based on average staffing costs has the dubious benefit of providing a budget surplus to inner city schools with a high staff turnover and numerous empty posts. But the effect of falling rolls in such areas had in the past also led to the merger of schools and relatively high staffing costs through the protection of posts and responsibility allowances after merger. These will put pressure on the delegated budgets of some schools and, even where treated as discretionary exceptions to the formula, they will have to be phased out after four years.

The draft formula originally produced for Avon, an LEA that spans all three types of catchment areas – urban, suburban and rural – was particularly criticized in these respects. Virtually all the inner city primary schools, and some of the most disadvantaged secondary schools in Bristol, stood to lose significant amounts of money under the original proposals (Guy and Menter, forthcoming). Only a concerted local campaign, which was subsequently featured on the front page of the *Times Educational Supplement*, produced changes. However, the same general tendency, albeit on a smaller scale, can still be detected in other authorities.

Some of those are authorities which have also had cuts in other forms of special funding, such as Section 11 grants (targeted at racially disadvantaged groups). Additionally, some of these same urban authorities have been charge-capped. An attempt to make a legal challenge to the 1990 charge-capping exercise, on the grounds that it would necessitate changes to delegated budgets already notified to governors, was unsuccessful. Although most of the seventeen charge-capped authorities eventually restricted their cuts to central services, and a few managed to avoid cutting education at all, they warned that future cuts would almost certainly hit delegated budgets. These are also the very LEAs where the promised freedom to tackle their chronic teacher shortage by paying market rates (see pp. 68–9) is likely to be made impossible by the budget restrictions imposed by the government.

Overall, there is little evidence that LMS will end the severe difficulties faced by inner city schools and some indication that, when combined with the effects of open enrolment on their pupil numbers, it will exacerbate them. In this connection, it is a matter of some concern that the promised publication of an HMI report on the effects of open enrolment on inner city schools has apparently been delayed (HMI, forthcoming).

CITY TECHNOLOGY COLLEGES

The government's plan for city technology colleges (CTCs), announced at the 1986 Conservative Party conference, was specifically targeted at inner city areas. However, Kenneth Baker's plan to establish a pilot programme of twenty CTCs by 1990 was already in some difficulties before the scheme was given a legislative basis in the Reform Act. Indeed, the wording of Section 105 of the Act itself represented some modification of the original proposal (Bristol Polytechnic Education Study Group, 1989). Subsequently, Baker's successors as Secretary of State, John MacGregor and Kenneth Clarke, have sometimes appeared lukewarm about the initiative, but the pressure to make it appear a success before the next general election remains strong.

Nevertheless, problems have continued to haunt the initiative and it now seems likely that only about fifteen colleges will be established, despite further modifications to the original scheme. In announcing CTCs, the government stated that it was seeking to work with 'interested individuals and organisations to establish with financial assistance from the Department of Education and Science a network of City Technology Colleges (CTCs) in urban areas'. Many of its preferred sites for the twenty pilot CTCs were in or adjacent to areas of inner city dereliction. In practice, both sponsors and sites have proved more difficult to find than was envisaged.

Whilst the failure to find appropriate sites, and the subsequent decision to accept sites in more suburban areas, could be blamed on obdurate Labour councils who refused to make inner city sites available, the problem of finding sponsors has been rather more embarrassing for the government. Not only were the costs of starting such schools 'woefully underestimated' by the DES, some major industrial companies like ICI very publicly dissociated themselves from the scheme, preferring to make their contribution to education via existing schools. Initially, it was only companies and individual entrepreneurs closely associated with a Thatcherite style of capitalism – e.g. Hanson Trust (Solihull), Dixons (Bradford) and Sir Philip Harris (Croydon and Docklands)

– who appeared to back the concept, and there were persistent rumours of ministerial arm-twisting (Ball, 1990). Press reports also pointed out that most of the early sponsors were major contributors to Conservative Party funds (Waterhouse, 1989). Even more damaging, just as the initiative appeared to be gathering momentum in 1990, were a scandal surrounding the purchase of the site for a so-called 'Green' CTC in Brighton·(*Education*, 1990a) and the spectacular crash of British and Commonwealth Holdings, another beneficiary of the Thatcherite boom in the City, which had been planning to sponsor the CTC in Bristol.

The various setbacks have meant that, by September 1990, only seven of the projected twenty CTCs are in operation. Two of these, in Croydon and Dartford, have incorporated existing schools and are phasing in the CTC approach over the next few years. This was an early attempt to expand the concept and thus to speed up the apparent progress of the initiative. Both those schools became CTCs with the agreements of their LEAs, but the two Haberdashers' Aske's schools in Lewisham, voluntary controlled schools whose governors under the leadership of the Haberdashers' Company sought CTC status, were only able to proceed after a series of legal challenges from the ILEA and its successor authority, Lewisham. In this case, the scheme was pushed through even though the parents at the girls' school voted against it in a ballot. Parental opposition was also ignored in the case of Sylvan School in Croydon, but a proposal to turn Riverside School in Bexley into a CTC was defeated by a concerted local campaign.

It is too early to tell in detail what CTC education will be like and whether there will be a distinctive and recognizable CTC ethos. When they were launched, it was claimed that:

> Their purpose will be to provide broadly-based secondary education with a strong technological element thereby offering a wider choice of secondary school to parents in certain cities and a surer preparation for adult and working life to their children. It is in our cities that the education system is at present under most pressure. (DES, 1986)

CTCs offered a 'new choice of school' with a modern curriculum and were seen as part of the solution to the perceived failure of many urban schools. Baker justified CTCs by pointing to what he perceived as the success of magnet and other specialist schools in the USA in transforming the achievement of inner city children and acting as 'beacons of excellence' to spur surrounding schools to make similar improvements.

Whether CTCs will actually provide more genuine opportunities for disadvantaged groups and whether they will succeed in stimulating improvements in other urban schools is far from clear. The original plans for siting this 'new choice of school' did suggest a concern with the particular needs of children in the inner city. Indeed, the decision to give them defined catchment areas, at a time when other schools were losing theirs, almost smacked of discredited policies of positive discrimination and implied a concern to avoid this particular initiative being colonized by groups well-served by other schools. The staff of the few CTCs already open claim that their intakes meet the requirement that they are to be socially representative of their areas, though a report drawn up for the DES apparently suggests that there is little concrete evidence to support their claims (Dean, 1990).

It was intended that the children at CTCs would not be selected on the basis of academic ability, but rather according to their orientation and motivation. This implied a shift in the definition of merit away from the narrowly academic one employed in the Assisted Places Scheme (Edwards *et al.*, 1989). Disadvantaged groups cannot therefore expect to be favoured indiscriminately, but only to the extent to which they display certain desired characteristics. The principal of Bradford CTC made this explicit recently in justifying a high acceptance rate for Asian applicants on the grounds that 'the strong work ethic associated with such families is exactly the sort of quality which we are looking for' (Lewis, 1990).

In terms of overall social composition, the very limited evidence available to date in relation to Kingshurst, the first CTC, which opened in Solihull in 1988, showed that its first two intakes had a higher proportion of children from partly skilled and unskilled backgrounds than from professional and intermediate groups, but the proportion of the latter was higher in the second intake than the first. There was also a higher proportion of ethnic minority children in the second intake (Walford, 1991). However, the changes reflected deliberate adjustments to the catchment area, designed to improve the social mix, a strategy reminiscent of the social engineering approach to the design of LEA comprehensive school catchment areas often criticized by the Right as limiting parental choice.

Meanwhile, at the same time as this CTC has felt it necessary to redraw its catchment area, some of the national leaders of the CTC movement are pressing for the removal of the catchment area concept altogether. Even without this, the strong competition for places that is already developing in some areas makes it difficult to predict what form selection will take in the future and the effects this will have on disadvantaged groups. Evidence from magnet schools in the USA and from the more traditional parts of the independent sector in the UK would suggest that popularity will make them increasingly selective, at least to the extent of excluding those groups who are perceived as being educationally 'at risk'. Walford and Miller (1991) argue, on the basis of their observations of education at Kingshurst in its first two years of operation, that CTCs will undoubtedly successfully sponsor members of the working class (or the 'deserving poor' as they once might have been called) out of their environment, but that they will have little positive impact on that environment and some negative consequences for those who remain in it.

Doubts are also being expressed about whether CTCs will, in practice, develop a distinctive style of education, beyond more extensive use of information technology than is possible in less well-equipped schools. These doubts partly arise from the fact that, notwithstanding its lack of mention in the Reform Act, they are to be required by their funding agreements to adhere to the National Curriculum. Some CTCs regard this as constraining their ability to specialize, even outside the normal teaching day, and as placing limits on the extent to which staff are willing to experiment with new curriculum models. Kingshurst and Djanogly CTC in Nottingham received much publicity for their plans to break with traditional styles of sixth-form provision. However, Walford and Miller (1991) regard the anticipated majority use of the International Baccalaureate rather than the Business and Technician Education Council (BTEC) qualifications at Kingshurst as legitimating the traditional hierarchy between academic and technical knowledge. They anyway feel that, as CTCs become increasingly popular, they will wish to move up the traditional hierarchy of esteem and thus 'deviate from [their original] role – as Kingshurst already appears to be doing'. Ball (1990) characterizes the CTCs as a terrain of struggle between the 'discourse of vocational progressivism' and that of the 'cultural restorationists', while the Gateshead CTC, which opened in September 1990, has Christian commitment and traditional values as key features of its appeal.

Meanwhile, though, the CTC concept has clearly had some effect on LEA provision. Some LEAs are establishing their own technology centres or planning to reorganize their own provision on a magnet school basis. Many more schools are rethinking their marketing strategy to attract pupils who might otherwise be tempted by the glossy high-tech image and generous initial resourcing levels of the CTCs. But, at the same time, CTCs are exacerbating the over-provision of school places in certain areas and many people blame the closure of Simon Digby School in Solihull, near the Kingshurst CTC, on the decision to site that CTC in a previously closed maintained school in an area of falling rolls (Walford and Miller, 1991). Simon Digby's application to avoid closure by seeking grant-maintained status was refused by the Secretary of State. Other LEAs, particularly some in south-east London where there is a heavy concentration of CTCs, are worried about the impact CTCs will have on enrolment patterns in their own schools and on their plans for rationalization.

Nevertheless, the direct effects of fewer than twenty CTCs on the system as a whole are likely to be limited, especially if they continue to be perceived by other schools as resourced at levels way above those that can be achieved by LEA-maintained schools. This is one reason why the concept of voluntary-aided CTCs is now being sponsored by the CTC Trust and tried out in Wandsworth. It means both that existing schools can be transformed without heavy initial costs and that, by retaining their links with the LEA, they will enter more directly into competition with other local schools.

GRANT-MAINTAINED SCHOOLS

The government claimed that grant-maintained schools would 'add a new and powerful dimension to the ability of parents to exercise choice within the publicly provided sector of education' and that 'parents and local communities [would] have new opportunities to secure the development of their schools in ways appropriate to the needs of their children and in accordance with their wishes, within the legal framework of the national curriculum' (DES, 1987b). It was seen as a means by which schools could become more responsive to their immediate clients and also as a way of reducing the power of left-wing Labour LEAs, particularly in urban areas.

The overall extent of opting out is difficult to assess at this stage. Mrs Thatcher's view that the majority of LEA-maintained schools would eventually opt out (Garner, 1987) was not upheld by the early evidence, but new incentives, and the extension of the scheme to make all primary schools eligible, were announced at the Conservative Party conference in October 1990 (Wintour and Bates, 1990). Although about half the LEAs in England and Wales contained schools that had sought grant-maintained status at that point, and nearly a third of LEAs contained at least one school where the change in status had been agreed, the 114 schools that had made moves in that direction represented only a very small proportion of all maintained schools (Fitz *et al.*, 1991). Nor has the government's expectation that the first schools to opt out would be from Labour-controlled urban LEAs been borne out in practice. Only about a third of the 48 schools whose transfer to grant-maintained status has so far been agreed are in Labour-controlled areas; indeed, it is the Conservative-controlled shire counties that have been amongst those most affected. Furthermore, by no means all the urban schools involved are in inner city areas.

Parental votes in over twenty schools have rejected plans to opt out and there have been other cases where LEAs (including left-wing urban LEAs) have persuaded school governing bodies not to proceed with a vote. There also appears to have been a recent slow-down in the number of applications for grant-maintained status. But even before the latest changes to the scheme, some LEAs were arguing that the government was bribing schools to go grant maintained by, for instance, granting GMSs 'over-generous initial capital grant allocations' compared with schools which remain in the LEA-maintained sector (Halpin and Fitz, 1990).

Predictions that if one school becomes grant maintained others in the locality may be tempted to do so are beginning to be borne out in practice. Of the first 32 LEAs that had GMSs within their boundaries, 11 already have more than one (Fitz *et al.*, 1991).

In situations where reorganization or school closure is planned, there is the possibility of serial applications for grant-maintained status. Thus, after Beechen Cliff school in Bath, Avon (see Chapter 1), had succeeded in its bid in order to avoid reorganization, the fear on the part of another school, Oldfield School, that it would now be earmarked for closure led that school to ballot on grant-maintained status (TES, 1990b).

Bath is a classic case of the problems that GMSs pose to an authority attempting to plan provision in accordance with its statutory duties and the directives of the Audit Commission about reducing surplus places. Avon, now a charge-capped authority, had 1,600 surplus places in Bath (and 17,000 in the LEA as a whole) and problems with sixth form viability. It had sought to close Beechen Cliff school and locate a sixth form college on the site. The Beechen Cliff parents voted 555 to 447 in favour of opting out on a 67 per cent turnout. The Secretary of State accepted the application, while rejecting Avon's reorganization plans. The authority argued that this was to put the interests of parents at one school above those of five other schools and that the Secretary of State had ignored the need to achieve economic and efficient education for the community as a whole.

At one stage, Avon LEA's legal challenge to the Secretary of State's decision looked like throwing the government's whole policy into confusion. An initial judicial review ruled in favour of the LEA and asked the Secretary of State to reconsider his decision to permit Beechen Cliff to opt out. This ruling suggested that the Secretary of State should weigh the case for opting out against the LEA's reorganization proposals and that he needed to consider the interests of all the parents and children in Bath. However, John MacGregor confirmed his original decision. A second judicial review took place in the Appeal Court, which ruled that it was up to the Secretary of State to decide the degree of importance to be given to different considerations and that it was not appropriate for Avon to pursue its differences of opinion with him via the courts. The school was therefore confirmed in its grant-maintained status. Avon's Director of Education has said that he will take the case to the European courts if necessary to 'defend the interests of and seek justice for all the children of Avon' (*Education*, 1990b).

The government originally stated that grant-maintained schools would not normally be permitted to change their character or admissions policies within five years of opting out, though it has recently announced its intention to remove this particular prohibition. This has been seen by critics as a backdoor means of reintroducing selection, and grant-maintained status has certainly been used to keep existing grammar schools selective. Thus, LEA-maintained grammar schools threatened with comprehensivization can immediately apply for grant-maintained status and receive a decision before any reorganization proposals are acted upon. They can then retain their existing selective character if they are successful in their bid to change their status. Some of the earliest schools to opt out came into this category and nineteen of the first 48 grant-maintained schools were selective schools.

On the other hand, John MacGregor showed some sensitivity to the charge that previously comprehensive schools would use their new status to introduce selection. In a number of cases where he agreed to the change in principle, he queried elements of the proposed admissions procedures. But in an ironic twist to the story, the governors of two schools on Stantonbury Campus, a model comprehensive school complex in Milton Keynes, decided to use the government's grant-maintained regulations to challenge a plan by their Conservative LEA to reintroduce grammar schools to the area. Although those plans were abandoned, the two schools are now grant-maintained comprehensive schools. While admiring the tactical skill of the governors, some supporters of comprehensive education have misgivings about this use of the Reform Act as it could be seen to legitimate what is essentially a reactionary policy.

Meanwhile, another debate which complicates traditional political divisions is developing around the question of minority schools, especially those for Muslim pupils. At the time of the Reform Bill, the (New Right) Hillgate Group (1987) argued that the government should encourage 'new and autonomous schools ... including Church schools of all denominations, Jewish schools, Islamic schools and such other schools as parents desire'. This was sometimes linked to a broader argument that 'the poor' had as much right to their 'own' schools as any other group. While the argument pointed in the direction of allowing the development of non-Christian voluntary-aided schools, something the government has always resisted, there were also suggestions that the same objective could be achieved either through state aid for independent religious schools or by the opting out of existing schools so that they could develop a religious or cultural distinctiveness. Marks (1990) has recently argued the case on the grounds of 'natural justice' and an all-party attempt was made in the House of Lords to remedy the failure of the Reform Act to meet this particular objective.

However, in general terms, it seems unlikely that grant-maintained status will produce diversity in the types of schooling available. There is certainly no evidence of that to date. Indeed, if Walford and Miller's argument about popular CTCs seeking to emulate the existing high-status parts of the system is also applicable to GMSs, then we can expect many of them to become increasingly academically selective in their intakes and conventional in their curricular approaches. Fitz *et al.* (1991) argue that, given the considerable number of 11 to 18, selective, voluntary and single-sex schools amongst the first GMS applications to be approved, the newly emergent sector as a whole may already be developing an image that appeals 'to parents seeking a "traditional" secondary schooling for their children'.

TEACHERS

Whether or not schools become more diversified in type, it does seem that the experience and conditions of work for teachers in those schools will become progressively differentiated. Within the maintained sector, at the same time that they have been coming to terms with implementing the National Curriculum and assessment arrangements, teachers have also been faced with increased uncertainty and vulnerability over their employment.

The formula funding of schools and the poll tax–capping of certain LEAs have led both separately and in combination to teacher redundancies in a number of areas. With regard to formula funding, schools with an 'expensive' staff have been hardest hit, particularly those that had been historically favoured by their LEA in terms of staffing. Some schools have had to make experienced teachers redundant, others have been unable to replace experienced staff who have retired. This is in spite of the 'safety net' arrangements which are supposed to reduce the immediate impact of substantial budgetary losses. Governing bodies are, for the first time, having to very carefully consider the salary a particular teacher would require before making appointments.

Teachers who are employed centrally by an LEA and those who work outside the statutory school age range are also particularly vulnerable in the climate of devolved budgets. A *Times Educational Supplement* survey of fifteen authorities carried out during the summer term of 1990 found 42 teachers who had been identified for compulsory redundancy (Nash, 1990). Many of these were members of supply teacher pools which were to be abolished or drastically diminished because of the new funding arrangements. When Avon was faced with poll tax–capping, its proposals for meeting a severely reduced budget included shedding many advisory and support teachers as well as nursery teachers throughout the county (see also Chapter 5). In the event the worst excesses have at least been staved off through drawing on contingency funds, but it is difficult to envisage how these posts can be protected for much longer.

These threats to teachers' employment have also demonstrated the new situation which the teaching unions are in. Whilst all unions have repeatedly voiced their dismay and anger at the repercussions of these financial arrangements, any industrial action in response to the cuts and their effects has been small-scale and short-term. The employment and trade union legislation brought in during the years of Conservative government has imposed severe constraints on the feasibility of strike action. So, for example, it would be illegal for any union to sanction national strikes over compulsory redundancies brought about by LMS (Blackburne *et al.*, 1990). In addition, the leadership of at least one of the traditionally militant unions, the National Union of Teachers, is actively discouraging strike action as an appropriate response in the new climate, preferring to rely instead on the persuasiveness of an advertising campaign to raise public awareness. Some strike action has been taken in particular localities, mostly in the form of token one-day protests.

Another aspect of increasing variation in teachers' conditions is that of pay. When teachers' negotiating rights were removed under the 1987 'settlement' (see Bristol Polytechnic Education Study Group, 1989), the then Secretary of State, Kenneth Baker, intimated that he would come forward with proposals for new negotiating procedures. In the event this responsibility fell to his successor, John MacGregor. In early summer 1990, Mr MacGregor announced his proposals, which whilst restoring to teachers the opportunity for collective bargaining simultaneously provided the opportunity for schools or LEAs to opt out of national pay settlements. Such local settlements would take the national agreements as a minimum and would provide for governing bodies or LEAs to create their own local markets. This was put forward partly as a response to the difficulties being faced in recruiting teachers in a number of geographical areas and in certain shortage subjects. The Secretary of State did not indicate where any 'extra' money might come from. It has been suggested that up to half of the grant-maintained schools will choose to opt out of the national arrangements (Blackburne and Dean, 1990). Many of the new CTCs are already operating their own pay structures as they come into being. Other aspects of competitive arrangements which are under consideration or being trialled include renewable contracts and performance-related pay, especially for headteachers. Stuart Sexton, a former adviser to Sir Keith Joseph and still very influential on government thinking, has called recently for all teachers to have personally negotiated contracts (Sexton, 1990a). However, in Spring 1991 the situation changed again, when Kenneth Clarke announced that teachers' pay will be subjected to consideration by a review body.

There is considerable political debate and some confusion about the extent of the crisis in teacher supply. Figures released by the Labour Party indicate that only one in three teachers still works in the classroom five years after qualifying. There are some metropolitan areas, particularly some London boroughs, that have been unable to fill vacancies in primary and secondary schools. But the government denies that there is a major crisis and has supported a number of strategies to alleviate such shortfalls of supply. These strategies have included the recruitment of teachers from overseas (including Europe and the Caribbean) and the development of alternative routes into teaching; that is, alternatives to four years of higher education. Amongst these alternatives the most radical is the licensing of untrained teachers or of teachers whose teaching qualifications are not recognized for the award of qualified teacher status by the DES. There remains considerable concern that licensed teachers, many of whom are expected to be members of ethnic minorities, will have a lower status, and that those who come into teaching without any pre-service training will find the strains and professional demands intolerable.

The reasons for the shortfall are several and complex. There is a huge number of teachers who are not teaching. There are certainly many who are leaving or considering alternative careers because of the changes in the nature of the work which result from the Education Reform Act. Nevertheless, it is interesting that in primary teaching at least, numbers of applicants for initial training both on B.Ed. and Post Graduate Certificate of Education (PGCE) courses appear to be holding up in spite of a demographic downturn in the number of 18-year-olds.

It seems likely that some major changes will soon occur within the initial training arrangements for teachers. Michael Fallon, the junior minister with responsibility for this area, has indicated that he is looking closely at existing arrangements. Given that he is a member of an influential ginger group of right-wing Conservative MPs ('The No Turning Back Group') and that a number of right-wing educational think-tanks have recently produced strident critiques of these arrangements (e.g. Lawlor, 1990), many teacher educators are bracing themselves for radical upheavals. It seems almost inevitable that there will be increased emphasis on school-based aspects of training.

In looking at the conditions and arrangements by which teachers are trained and employed the extent of the effects of restructuring are emerging. In this context the re-emergence of a debate about the need for a general teaching council is particularly significant. The Labour Party education spokesperson, Jack Straw, is a strong advocate of such a council, arguing that it would have very positive effects on the profession, both ensuring the maintenance of teaching quality and protecting teachers from the worst effects of competition and division within the teaching force.

SPECIAL EDUCATIONAL NEEDS

At the time the Reform Bill was passing through Parliament, some concessions were won on the issue of special educational needs, particularly in relation to the National Curriculum. However, as we have already seen, the approach to budgetary provision for special educational needs under LMS has varied considerably from authority to authority (Lee, 1990). The decision by some LEAs to follow the government's preference for simple formulae, particularly by using the take-up of free school meals as a measure for special educational needs, can have particularly striking effects. Levacic (1990), for example, shows how an LEA that used free meals and pupil turnover as indicators created considerable changes in the distribution of funds, whereas another LEA, with a relatively sophisticated special needs index, brought about a distribution more in line with earlier subjective judgements of educational need.

When the Bill was being discussed there was considerable concern that, under open enrolment and LMS, a school would 'have to balance the attraction of gaining additional funds by taking children with special educational needs against the possibility that the school [would] become stigmatized and thus face a reduction in its basic income through the effects of falling rolls' (Bristol Polytechnic Education Study Group, 1989). While it is too early to get a clear indication of how schools will resolve this dilemma, school-based research by Gold *et al.* (1990) demonstrates that teachers are very conscious of this dilemma as they make decisions about their special needs provision.

Meanwhile, the House of Commons Select Committee on Education, Science and Arts (1990) has argued that LMS, opting out, and other provisions of the Reform Act are likely to undermine some of the progress made in integrating pupils with special educational needs into mainstream schools. The committee feels that the LMS formulae adopted by many LEAs in relation to special needs are too narrow to bring into schools the additional resources which are required to enable them to cope with the full range of educational needs identified by the Warnock Report (see Chapter 2). Furthermore, even those needs that are recognized in the formulae may not offer sufficient enticement to schools to take pupils with those needs. The Committee suspects that many schools will feel that the market consequences of doing so would be to make the school less attractive to those parents whose children provide the bulk of the pupils whose numbers drive the funding formula. In those circumstances, children with special educational needs may well become concentrated in those schools which have difficulties in recruiting other pupils. It remains to be seen whether the government's latest circular (7/91) on special needs in the context of LMS will do anything to mitigate such tendencies.

CONCLUSIONS

At present, it seems more likely that the Reform Act will produce greater differentiation between schools on a linear scale of quality and esteem than the positive diversity that some of its supporters hoped for. At the time the Act was passed, we pointed to the possibility that a new hierarchy of schools might emerge, running from elite independent schools at the pinnacle through CTCs, grant-maintained schools and voluntary schools, to LEA-maintained schools at the base (Bristol Polytechnic Education Study Group, 1989). Walford and Miller (1991) now claim that while comprehensive schools attempted to overcome the historic links between diversity of provision and inequalities of class and gender 'the CTCs have played a major part in re-legitimizing inequality of provision for different pupils'. Indeed, they suggest that the 'inevitable result' of the concept of CTCs, especially when coupled with GMSs and LMS, is 'a hierarchy of schools with the private sector at the head, the CTCs and GMSs next, and the various locally managed LEA schools following'. Whether or not 'inevitable', there are certainly some signs of a hierarchy developing, thus casting doubt on the assertion of Bob Dunn, the Minister of State during the Act's passage, that 'more and more specialised, differentiated schools' could develop 'without any one being regarded as inferior to the others' (*Education*, 1988).

Overall, there is little evidence that the Education Reform Act is providing a structure that will ensure equality of opportunity for all pupils and some evidence that the reforms further disadvantage those unable to compete in the market they are intended to foster. This raises particular issues for the predominantly working-class and black populations who inhabit the inner cities. While they have never gained an equitable share of educational resources under past policies, the abandonment of planning in favour of the market seems highly unlikely to provide a solution. There is a real possibility that an educational underclass will be created in Britain's inner cities, increasingly isolated from the political movements that have campaigned for over a century to provide and improve the education service as a whole. The Act is likely to increase structural inequalities rather than challenge them, while fostering the belief that its championing of choice provides genuinely equal opportunities for all those individuals who wish to benefit from them. For those members of disadvantaged groups who are not sponsored out of schools at the bottom of the status hierarchy, either on grounds of exceptional academic ability or alternative definitions of merit, the outlook is particularly bleak. As Eric Bolton, Her Majesty's Senior Chief Inspector, wrote in his second annual report, looking back on 1988-9:

> Sadly, less able pupils are much more likely to experience the poor and the shoddy than the more able: a worryingly persistent feature of English education at all levels. (HMI, 1990)

Whether the tendencies identified in this chapter will escalate or be checked in the coming years is partly dependent on the result of the next general election and on the extent to which the opposition parties develop coherent alternative policies (see also Chapter 8). Stuart Sexton (whose pamphlet on teachers' pay was mentioned earlier) has recently suggested that increasing numbers of schools will opt out of LEA control over the next four to five years, and that if the Conservatives win the next two elections we will not have LEAs running education in ten years' time (Sexton, 1990b). Certainly, some of the developments outlined here point in that direction. Calderdale, a Labour-controlled metropolitan LEA implementing drastic expenditure cuts and now facing a further loss of revenue through the opting-out of its two grammar schools, has already expressed doubts about its ability to survive as an LEA even in present circumstances (*Education*, 1990c). If the Conservatives do not win further terms of office, a new government could be faced with a truly chaotic situation. Any government genuinely committed to social justice would then have to find new ways of planning the education system so that it served the needs of the least-advantaged members of society rather than merely those well-placed to play the market. Whatever the declared motives of the current restructuring of the system, there is certainly no evidence yet that it is serving that end.

REFERENCES

• Ball, S. (1990) *Politics and Policymaking in Education*. London: Routledge.

• Ball, S. and Bowe, R. (1990) 'The spirit is willing but the flesh is weak': An exploration of LMS in one secondary school. Paper presented at St Hilda's College, Oxford.

• Blackburne, L. (1988) Peers back policy on open enrolment. *Times Educational Supplement*, 13 May.

• Blackburne, L. and Dean, C. (1990) Schools may opt out of national pay settlements. *Times Educational Supplement*, 4 May.

• Blackburne, L., Dean, C. and Lodge, B. (1990) NUT caught in cleft stick over strikes. *Times Educational Supplement*, 20 April.

• Bristol Polytechnic Education Study Group (1989) Restructuring the Education System? In Bash, L. and Coulby, D. (eds) *The Education Reform Act: Competition and Control*. London: Cassell.

• Dean, C. (1990) CTC selectors face an impossible task. *Times Educational Supplement*, 21 September, p. 1.

• DES (1986) *City Technology Colleges: A New Choice of School*. London: DES.

• DES (1987a) *Admission of Pupils to Maintained Schools*. London: DES.

• DES (1987b) *Grant Maintained Schools: Consultation Paper*. London: DES.

• *Education* (1988) Mr Dunn's version of morality and the curriculum. 8 July.

• *Education* (1990a) The leaves of the green CTC turn brown and fall off. 4 May.

• *Education* (1990b) Final submissions in the Beechen Cliff case. 4 May.

• *Education* (1990c) Opting out reaper triggers fears of an educational Doomsday. 17 August.

• Edwards, A., Fitz, J. and Whitty, G. (1989) *The State and Private Education: An Evaluation of the Assisted Places Scheme*, Lewes: Falmer Press.

• Fitz, J., Halpin, D. and Power, S. (1991) Grant maintained schools: a third force in education? *Forum*, January.

• Garner, R. (1987) Mrs Thatcher enthuses over opting out proposals. *Times Educational Supplement*, 18 September.

• Gold, A., Bowe, R. and Ball, S. (1990) Special educational needs in a new context: micropolitics, money, and education for all. Paper presented to the Annual Conference of the British Educational Research Association.

• Guy, W. and Menter, I. (forthcoming) Local management of schools: who benefits? In Gill, D. and Mayor, B. (eds) *Racism and*

Education: Strategies for Change. Milton Keynes: Open University Press.

• Halpin, D. and Fitz, J. (1990) Local education authorities and the grant-maintained schools policy. Paper presented to the Annual Conference of the British Educational Research Association.

• Hillgate Group (1987) *The Reform of British Education*. London: Claridge Press.

• HMI (1990) *Standards in Education 1988-9: The Annual Report of the Senior Chief Inspector*. London: HMSO.

• HMI (forthcoming) *A Survey of the Effects of Open Enrolment on Smaller Inner City and Urban Schools*. London: Department of Education and Science.

• House of Commons Select Committee on Education, Science and Arts (1990) *Staffing for Pupils with Special Educational Needs*, London: HMSO.

• Hugill, B. (1990) Government lets parents choose schools by race. *The Observer*, 22 April.

• Johnson, R. (1989) Thatcherism and English education: breaking the mould or confirming the pattern? *History of Education* 18(2).

• Knight, B. (1990) Research on local management of schools. Paper presented to the Annual Conference of the British Educational Research Association.

• Lawlor, S. (1990) *Teachers Mistaught?* London: Centre for Policy Studies.

• Lee, T. (1990) Special educational needs and social disadvantage under LMS: present issues and future implications. *Advisory Centre for Education Bulletin* 35, May/June.

• Levacic, R. (1990) An analysis of differences between historic and formula school budgets: evidence from LEA submissions and from detailed study of two LEAs. Paper presented to the Annual Conference of the British Educational Research Association.

• Lewis, J. (1990) Bradford CTC responds. Letter in *Education*, 1 June.

• Marks, J. (1990) Let natural justice be done. *Times Educational Supplement*, 17 August.

• Nash, I. (1990) Drastic LMS job cuts confirmed by councils. *Times Educational Supplement*, 1 June.

• Sexton, S. (1990a) *Teachers' Pay*. London: Institute of Economic Affairs.

• Sexton, S. (1990b) *Today* programme. BBC Radio 4, 6 September.
• Spencer, D. (1989) Fund set up to challenge Greenwich court ruling. *Times Educational Supplement*, December 29.
• TES (1990a) Budget move may force cuts in central services. *Times Educational Supplement*, 10 August.
• TES (1990b) Governors defy Avon in opt-out fight. *Times Educational Supplement*, 3 August.
• Walford, G. (1991) City Technology Colleges: a private magnetism? In Walford, G. (ed.) *Private Schooling: Tradition, Change and Diversity*. London: Paul Chapman Publishing.
• Walford, G. and Miller, H. (1991) *City Technology Colleges*. Milton Keynes: Open University Press.
• Ward, D. (1989) Heads for finance needed next spring. *The Guardian*, 25 April.
• Waterhouse, R. (1989) Mounting costs of Baker's beacons. *The Independent*, 29 June.
• Weekes, W. (1987) Tory fury at Heath attack on 'divisive' schools Bill. *Daily Telegraph*, 2 December.
• Wintour, P. and Bates, S. (1990) All schools get opt-out rights. *The Guardian*, 11 October.

5

Local Management of Schools

Leslie Bash

LMS is an important reform, with significant implications and opportunities for schools. The Government and LEAs will be monitoring its introduction carefully, so that any necessary changes to national and local policy can be made in the light of experience. (DES, 1990)

The biggest change since my last newsletter is the introduction of what is grandly known as local management. This is a joyous misnomer for a system whereby I manage the Government's curriculum and the Government's testing programme with a sum of money determined by the Government's formula. (Wragg, 1990)

INTRODUCTION

It may be of more than passing relevance to know that this chapter began to take shape in the aftermath of one of the worst riots that London has witnessed this century. The anti-poll tax rally which preceded the actions of some fringe left groups, in turn eliciting an unequivocal response from the Metropolitan Police, was merely the latest in a succession of vehement protests against the community charge. Such demonstrations of collective feeling were notable for their abandonment of party politics: the crowds comprised adherents of all the major groupings, as well as those with no particular allegiance at all. While the protests signified the inequitable nature of a totally regressive tax, they also represented a deep frustration with the way central government has increasingly tightened its grip over local affairs. It would be a mistake to conclude that the poll tax as such was the result of political incompetence and miscalculation – on the contrary, it may be seen as part of a coherent strategy to counter alternative bases for political action.

It is against this background that there must be some consideration of the changes wrought by the 1988 Act in relation to the management of resources in schools. Originally known as 'local financial management', it was soon realized that it was more than just an alteration in accounting procedures; the new system was more far-reaching in its consequences, since it sought to shift responsibility for resourcing away from LEAs towards governing bodies and headteachers. Local management of schools (LMS) was to be the panacea for headteachers frustrated at having to become involved in seemingly excessive local authority bureaucracy every time a new supply of exercise books – or a supply teacher – was needed. It offered autonomy at a time when the imposition of the National Curriculum was about to take it away. On the other hand, as will be demonstrated in this chapter, however 'well-managed' schools become under LMS, glaring contradictions have now appeared, threatening to undermine other aspects of the 1988 Act. At this juncture, a résumé of LMS is appropriate. As stated in Bash and Coulby (1989):

> Under the terms of Section 33 of the Act, all LEAs will be required to submit to the Secretary of State schemes of financial delegation covering all county and voluntary secondary schools and primary schools with 200 or more pupils on roll.... The delegated budgets are to include staffing, books and equipment and other goods and services used by the schools (including examination fees), and day-to-day premises costs, including rent and rates. (Bristol Polytechnic Education Study Group, 1989, pp. 35–6)

This means that governing bodies will have the power to make decisions on spending within the limits of budgets delegated to their schools. Other aspects of expenditure are earmarked for particular purposes, such as central administration, inspection and advisory services and home to school transport, and cannot be vired by governors. Central to the process of financial delegation is the notion of formula funding, whereby the major determinant of a school's budget is the number and ages of pupils on roll, with the possibility of other factors being taken into account (special needs, small rural schools, etc.). It should, perhaps, be noted that formula funding now applies to all schools, even if they are not yet under LMS. Furthermore, some schools which are not locally managed may still have delegated budgets, which means that although virement between different areas of expenditure may take place, a surplus of funds cannot be carried over from one financial year to the next, and would, therefore, have to revert to the local authority.

Crucially, under LMS, school governors gain the considerable powers of hiring and firing staff, as well as determining their number (Bristol Polytechnic Education Study Group, 1989, pp. 36–8). It is this last area which has provided the main focus of attention, since teachers' salaries constitute by far the biggest item (about 63 per cent) of schools' budgets. The delegated budget for each school will be based upon the LEA's *average* teaching costs rather than the school's *actual* teaching costs. One major consequence of this is that schools with stable, long-serving staffs will have to spend more of their budgets on teachers' salaries than those with high turnover of probationers.

NEW MANAGEMENT STRUCTURES

For those who run schools the main attraction of LMS is clear. In an interview, the head of a pilot school for LMS cited the biggest advantage as the possession of a sense of freedom and flexibility. On the other hand, it demanded the appointment of someone who could be trained as a bursar to administer LMS within the school. A list of the duties associated with the post gives some flavour of the responsibilities to be assumed by most schools after 1 April 1990. A bursar:

- Manages the School's computerised administrative system.
- Carries out all office duties required, including correspondence, children's registration and records, filing, etc.
- Supervises the day-to-day running of the school, organising school visits, booking buses, reception of visitors.
- Responsibility for manual staff and arrangements to cover absences.
- Under the supervision of the Head Teacher, is responsible for training, work standards, attendance and

discipline of all non-teaching staff.

- Prepares information for management reports, statistical returns.
- Required to act as Clerk to the Governors, Sub-Committees of Governors, School Management Team including circulation of agenda papers, preparing notes of meetings, preparing correspondence and implementing decisions.
- Prepares draft annual revenue budget for approval of Head Teacher and Governing Body.
- Advises Head Teacher and Governing Body of financial implications of developments, proposals to correct variations.
- Administers purchase of supplies and equipment within the budget.
- Prepares weekly and monthly returns and claims for grants, allowances and expenses, etc. Where possible, answers queries from staff on pay and conditions of service.
- Supervises the receipt of cash, reconciliation of cash accounts and use of bank accounts.
- Supervises school caretaking and cleaning staff.
- Receives regular reports from the caretaker on the state of repair of buildings, fixtures and fittings; authorises minor repairs.
- Invites tenders for maintenance and services. Ensures contractors perform duties according to the contract. Reviews contracts and recommends termination/renewal to the Head.
- Contacts building inspector in the case of suspected major defects.
- Reviews and maintains the school insurance policies.
- Ensures that the provisions of the Health and Safety at Work Act are observed and that the accident book is properly completed.
- Ensures that pupils receive first aid and attention for minor injuries and illnesses. Liaises with the Area Health Authority on medical arrangements in the School and maintains all administration connected with school medicals, health records, etc. (Christchurch C. of E. Primary School, 1990)

And all this working a 36-hour week (over 39 weeks) for less than £6,500 per annum. Elsewhere in the primary sector, a number of schools have jointly hired the services of a bursar who will offer such expertise as is needed but leave day-to-day administration to the schools themselves. Thus, despite the appointment of bursars, headteachers still find they have many financial responsibilities. Rather, what has happened is the creation of administrative 'departments' within schools, and, as a consequence, an increase in the overall quantity of administration. Those who might have predicted a proliferation of bureaucracy as a result of LMS will not be disappointed by what has emerged in this Wiltshire primary school.

Yet LMS has undoubtedly enabled many headteachers and governing bodies to feel that they have gained a measure of control over the spending for their schools. If a repair has to be carried out on the fabric of the school building there is no longer a need to await the go-ahead from the LEA – something which might take months, even years. Instead, the headteacher could probably take executive action and call in a local contractor with the knowledge that the necessary money to pay for the job is immediately available. Even though a school's budget will, in theory, take into account diverse aspects of school expenditure, the possibility of being able to vire funds from one area to another is extremely attractive. As one headteacher has remarked:

> Our experience of Local Management has been that there are three main advantages. Firstly, virement over budget headings gives greater flexibility – being able to manipulate money so that it is used where it is most needed. Secondly, we're no longer limited to having to spend all the budget by the end of the financial year – an enormous advantage and thirdly, we 'save money by accident'. Sometimes we are unable to appoint a member of staff or a department head leaves and is temporarily replaced by a supply teacher. Money is 'accidentally' saved and is ours to spend. (Kent County Council, 1990, p. 40)

There are, undoubtedly, other changes to the structure of management in schools which have been associated with LMS and which also reflect the imposition of the National Curriculum. Such changes have emphasized the importance of 'flexibility, teamwork, communication, and consultation' (Roberts and Ritchie, 1990, p. 21), demonstrating, paradoxically, that

> schools which succeed in the new competitive environ-
> ment . . . are likely to be those where the collaborative acti-
> vities of planning, goal-setting, prioritising and self-
> evaluation are most highly developed. (Roberts and Ritchie,
> 1990, p. 21)

Local management, then, is as much about the internal organization of the teaching and learning process as it is about balancing
the books. However, the books do have to be balanced and LMS,
in practice, has meant the imposition of 'cost consciousness',
the elimination of 'waste' and obtaining 'value for money'. Heads
are required to monitor the use of energy in their schools and
to ensure as far as possible that the school buildings produce
income from lettings. Even here, some outside groups may
receive preferential consideration: an adult education keep-fit
class does not need the same amount of heating to be provided
as one for elementary bookkeeping. Evidently, this kind of thinking is what is now required in order for schools to be able to
exercise the autonomy which they have been lacking for so long.
If, in the future, schools find it difficult to make ends meet
they will only have themselves to blame; it will simply be the
consequence of bad housekeeping. If, on top of that, published
test results are unimpressive (see Chapter 3), this will confirm,
in the eyes of parents of prospective pupils, that such schools
are headed for eventual closure and they will seek a better service
elsewhere.

In general, then, the broad swathe of opinion among headteachers suggests that LMS is something of a curate's egg. While
the disadvantages are seen to outweigh the advantages, when
all is said and done LMS has to be lived with. This may, of
course, be the case, although a change of government, as with
other aspects of the Act, could lead to abolition or modification.
Schools, after the self-teaching exercise undertaken by those
piloting LMS, are now awash with a multitude of guides to local
management – from the DES, the LEAs, the educational press,
and book publishers. The ideology of managerialism has now
firmly taken its place in schools, accompanied by the more concrete trappings of commercial life. Thus, alongside the BBC and
Nimbus microcomputers in the classroom, the IBM-type PC is

making an appearance as a key administrative tool in the establishment of a management system.

THE EXPERTS' VIEW

So, LMS has considerable support among those headteachers who, in the past, have felt constrained in their ability to run their schools in an efficient and effective manner. From their position, there need be no more interference and obstruction by the bureaucrats at County Hall. Here, belief in the folk-devil of the LEA bureaucrat coincides with Conservative opinion which has singled out the apparatus of local government as being particularly obstructive in the quest for efficiency, value for money, and the promotion of the goals of individuals and their families. With the power of LEA bureaucracy held in check, and, perhaps, diminished, the introduction of LMS would appear to deal yet another blow at the stranglehold over enterprise and initiative created and sustained by municipal socialism.

There ought, therefore, to be additional outright support for LMS from that group of professionals who have gained praise from government in their efforts to modernize industry: the management consultants. Such people, with their roots in the world of accountancy, have apparently shown how inefficient practices can be eliminated in the quest for greater profitability and competitiveness.

Consequently, at this point in the assessment of LMS it would be helpful in practice to consider some of the observations made by Thompson (1990), two years after the publication of a report on LMS (DES, 1988) by Coopers & Lybrand – now Coopers & Lybrand Deloitte – of which he is the partner responsible for education and training consultancy. In his view, the effective implementation of LMS required a significant increase in resources – which appears not to have occurred. The question of 'gainers' and 'losers' under formula funding (see pp. 68-71) is raised as an important issue, if only because of the perceptions of unfairness which have resulted. Likewise, the issue of staffing costs is seen as one which may have serious consequences for many schools (see pp. 70-1). Moreover, the essential factor is, that for a school

> to attempt to develop any sort of plan without full reference to its resource implications will be of little value; and it

is equally pointless to consider resource issues without reference to what the school is trying to do. (Thompson, 1990, p. 14).

A further question concerning the implications of LMS for local authorities is raised by Thompson. The Coopers & Lybrand report (DES, 1988) suggested that if LEAs no longer had to deal with issues of individual school management then they could be left to concentrate on their 'strategic role' as planners of overall educational provision. Yet the emphasis given by the 1988 Act to opting out and open enrolment plainly undermines this new role. If the market is given prominence through the operation of 'parent power' LEAs will in fact have little strategic authority left at all. Indeed, it would be rather like asking the generals to plan a battle campaign where the privates are entitled to fight in any manner they like. In addition, with different LEAs retaining different proportions of the schools' budget for central administration it would be difficult to make any kind of overall judgement as to the effective performance of such a role.

These observations by Coopers & Lybrand merit some comment since the advice of this firm of consultants was significantly influential in the adoption of LMS as government policy. Having helped light the fuse there is now some concern about the force of the explosion. It does illustrate the problematic nature of the involvement of technical expertise in pursuit of ideological goals. It may well be that Coopers & Lybrand, together with other experts in management, felt that local management in education would ultimately result in better quality and a more just distribution of resources. However, such a conclusion might rest on certain assumptions regarding justice which are not necessarily held by government, and it is government, not consultants, which enacts policy.

FORMULA FUNDING

In addition there is a need to examine the impact of formula funding. Despite the potential unity within the education system offered by the National Curriculum, the existing disparities between primary and secondary schools in terms of resources are about to widen. With at least 75 per cent of LEAs' overall budgets for schools paid over in age-weighted pupil units, and, in practice, wide variations above this figure, it is scarcely surprising that at secondary level large sixth forms will, more than ever, be the yardstick for remuneration. Since each pupil over the age of 16 will be bringing in a significantly higher sum to the school, a headteacher with only a basic understanding of profit and loss is bound to want to retain as many children as possible until they are 18. One such head has even managed to run a thriving Certificate of Pre-Vocational Education (CPVE) course for non-A-level pupils when CPVE elsewhere has been less than popular (Porter, 1990). This will, if pursued, pose yet another threat to LEA reorganization of secondary schooling, especially if some kind of tertiary system is envisaged (see Chapter 7).

The platitude that the foundations of learning are laid in the early years of schooling will, therefore, begin to sound somewhat hollow. In short, formula funding, as it is currently practised, does not appear to have had the effect of channelling the necessary resources through to the primary sector.

THE REALITY OF UNDER-RESOURCING

So, as might be expected, the flexibility brought about by LMS, combined with the resoluteness of a government determined to curb public expenditure both centrally and locally through poll tax–capping, has brought about downward pressures to pursue cheapness. When an important expenditure decision might result in 'robbing Peter to pay Paul' that decision may have to be taken only after a thorough costing procedure. With the staffing of schools constituting the biggest single item of expenditure, few people have been surprised by the increasing focus upon long-serving teachers and the possibilities for redundancy and early retirement. However, although persistently denied by the DES, LEAs and their schools have also had to face the prospect of severe teacher shortages, thus prompting statements of the following kind:

> We are facing a paradoxical situation of which I am sure you are aware and which requires careful consideration. Governors are being given greater powers to grant early retirement at a time when the recruitment and retention of teachers is becoming an issue in Wiltshire. It would be ironical if we encountered simultaneously a greater number

of retirements with enhancements and the need to provide expensive relocation packages to recruit teachers into Wiltshire. (Wiltshire County Council, 1990, p. 1)

This potential contradiction is further sharpened when seen in the context of the demands made by the National Curriculum. The growing cynicism among headteachers is reflected in this item from a recent newsletter to the parents of children at the primary school previously cited:

> Do you know of any qualified teacher prepared to work for up to 56 hours a week starting at £9,000 (rising after 11 years to a more reasonable level) who is experienced at teaching the core curriculum, Maths, English and Science as well as Technology, History, Geography, Music, Art, P.E. and R.E. with expert classroom management techniques and highly tuned interpersonal social skills? No overtime is payable and applicants must expect to spend considerable periods during the children's holidays on training days, classroom preparation and professional development. (Christchurch School, 1990, p. 2)

However, the negative impact of LMS upon resources available to schools goes beyond what is contained in devolved budgets. For example, it was reported that a threat was posed to school library services as a consequence of some LEAs preparing to give the money (retained centrally for library provision) to schools ... and launch the library service as a commercial operation (Pyke, 1990, p. 5). At a time of low spending by LEAs on books and resources, and given the promotion of resource-based learning by the National Curriculum and GCSE, the threat to library services seemed to border on the insane, highlighting a clear contradiction.

Given the reality of under-resourcing, LMS manifests itself as yet a further means of maintaining divisiveness in the English education system. Whatever the arguments are for the devolution of budgetry powers to individual schools, and there would be few who would not support a considerable degree of autonomy in this area, there is little to commend a policy which threatens the fabric of cohesive LEA provision. There is little doubt that the governing bodies of many schools, even relatively small primary ones, will begin to discuss moves towards grant-maintained status, especially in those authorities which have retained 35 per cent or more of funding for central spending. In one primary school where £50,000 was retained for 'central administration costs' the headteacher felt that the services offered in return were of poor quality when compared with what might be purchased elsewhere on the open market (Messor, 1990).

LMS in practice has, as has been anticipated, become associated with a growing and intense cynicism. The process by which the cake is divided has tended to eclipse any questions concerning the size of the cake itself. In the week before LMS came on stream for many schools one headteacher remarked that the training sessions provided by his LEA were very good, having taught him the essentials of budget preparation and operation. However,

> What they could not do was to make balancing the books a real pleasure. My consternation that I had an insufficient allowance to maintain standards, never mind expand, has been shared by virtually all my colleagues. (Quoted in Vaughan, 1990, p. 27).

With many local authorities having set lower than expected community charges, or having suffered capping, this state of affairs is hardly surprising. Even if the financing of education takes into account inflation there is a good chance of severe underestimation. Average spending per annum on books and equipment for primary schoolchildren is reckoned to be £23 each, or, when broken down, 'less than the weekly cost of three Mars bars' (Bates, 1990). If that is the case, LMS may be correctly viewed as no more than an exercise in the removal of responsibility for declining resources from the LEA to the school. Once more, a situation is arising where the victim – the school – is to be held ultimately to blame for its own fate, and parents will be left to judge.

PRESENTING THE PRODUCT

Perhaps this highlights, more than anything, the effects of LMS upon schools. There is the freedom for headteachers and governing bodies to conduct their own affairs in the manner thought fit, so long as centrally prescribed demands are met. There is the freedom to be enterprising and 'entrepreneurial' – and the freedom to lose pupils and go 'bankrupt'. The headteacher cited earlier (Messor, 1990) decided that advertising in the window of a local building society, with a display of the best of the children's work, was a good way of pulling in the customers (while at the same time diverting them from other, less enterprising institutions). Such an approach to school management has received the seal of approval from the Marketing Officer of Bradford City Council's Education Department:

> The 1988 Education Reform Act allows parents and pupils to have greater flexibility over their choice of school, and parents and members of the business and other communities to have greater representation on governing bodies. Schools will ignore the needs of these customers at their peril. With budgets largely being calculated according to pupil numbers and schools becoming increasingly accountable for their spending, never has the necessity for attracting and retaining customers been greater [*sic*]. This will only be done effectively by ... marketing. (Clayton, 1990, p. 19)

The implication of the marketing mode of operation is not only to ensure that publicity is given to the positive aspects of a school's activities but that no publicity at all is given to negative aspects. With an increasingly high profile being given to bullying, secondary schools where bullying is prevalent will hardly wish to highlight this aspect in their prospectuses – especially where there are falling rolls. Nor will schools wish to publicize high incidences of drug-taking, or of gas emissions from adjacent factories. On the contrary, such information is likely to be withheld or glossed over, prompting some futuristic school management to adopt a rather aggressive campaign along the lines of:

> Why go to Meanstaff Comprehensive where every bully has his way? Send your child to Happy Street High School for contentment, creativity and curriculum success. (Combes, 1990, p. 20)

THE EFFECTS ON THE TEACHING PROFESSION

LMS may well have had the effect of thrusting schools into the 'real' world of responsibility and accountability, but what of the effects on an already demoralized teaching force? With their collective bargaining rights taken away and with the expectation that they perform an ever-increasing number of tasks in and out of the classroom, they can no longer look forward to uniform conditions of service across the country. Under LMS, schools are free to adopt – or not to adopt – LEA policies on industrial relations. As a consequence, schools may be able to attract and retain valuable staff – or lose them altogether. But the pressures towards cheapness have resulted in a not altogether unexpected wariness over permanent contracts. Incentive posts may be available, but often only for a limited time-period, and will be increasingly related to specific tasks to be performed within the school. Of course, the market may dictate that some posts in primary schools (for the core areas of the curriculum) will have to be permanently designated above Main Professional Grade (MPG), but these are only likely to attract 'A' allowances.

As schools become increasingly driven by the demands of the 1988 Act other contradictions expose themselves. Ironically, the more that teachers wish to increase their understanding of curriculum and managerial issues through in-service education of teachers (INSET) the more they are likely to put a strain on the devolved budgets of their schools. In a less competitive era, with greater commitment to the further professional and academic development of teachers, those who made application to local authorities for course funding generally perceived this as a legitimate, indeed laudable action. Today, however, under LMS, staff development is constrained by instrumentality, and a teacher who seeks to secure financial support from her school for an award- bearing course, no matter how 'relevant', will either have it refused because of other pressing needs or else will feel guilty – especially if she also happens to be the headteacher! There is, therefore, an increased reluctance to support certain kinds of INSET activity, especially if associated with diplomas or higher degrees. The knock-on effects for the main providers of INSET are likely to be substantial, with teacher education institutions having to cut many of their courses, even when there is a good deal of support both from LEAs and individual schools.

THE CHALLENGE TO LOCAL DEMOCRACY

It is now apparent that the contradictions and conflicts experienced as a result of the operation of LMS reflect much more fundamental divisions over the control of local affairs, and not just education. The politics of the last decade indicate the unwillingness of central government to tolerate opposition to its policies, and as a result local democracy seems to be increasingly at risk.

Superficially, it seems paradoxical that the implementation of the local management of schools, with its attendant appeal to notions of freedom and accountability, should be accompanied by an erosion of local democracy. At a somewhat less than superficial level, it is perfectly consistent with the ideology of individualism and the lack of emphasis upon collective life in society. Although this aspect is dealt with throughout the book, it is of vital importance to the theme of this chapter to emphasize the continued emasculation of local government. It is now evident that the days of the county councils are numbered (Dean, 1990). The Conservative right has proposed that practically all local services should be taken over by the district councils (and, in a separate critique of the role of county councils, the Labour Party – in the opposite direction – has suggested the creation of regional councils). While the abolition of the Greater London Council and the metropolitan counties did not affect the provision of education, it did at least provide the precedent for the removal of the rest of the county councils and thus the removal of problematic LEAs. Whether the provision of education would then fall to the district councils, or whether grant-maintained status would be extended to all schools, remains to be seen, although the latter would seem to be the more likely scenario, given the probable ineffectiveness of small district councils as LEAs.

It is only in this context that the poll tax and its attendant 'charge capping' can now be fully understood. The irony of this in relation to the professed policy of increasing local account-ability is clear. More pertinently in relation to this chapter, the conflict between a central government determined to limit the revenue raised by local authorities and the obligations imposed by the Education Reform Act upon LEAs, is quite open. Put simply, the heavy hand of the Environment Secretary has appeared to make it impossible to implement the changes demanded by the Education Secretary. Many have contemplated severe cuts in educational expenditure, including the closure of those services which do not appear to impact upon the implementation of the National Curriculum. Chris Saville, Director of Education for Avon LEA, predicted closure of all nurseries, the multicultural support centre, and the disappearance of school and FE curriculum development work (Castle, 1990). However, at the time of writing, the extent to which charge-capping has merely been used by hard-pressed local authorities as a propaganda weapon against central government, rather than as a genuine reason for having to make expenditure cuts, is not at all clear.

Given that education constitutes the single biggest item of expenditure by local authorities, the prospect of many more schools opting out may signal their eventual demise. While this would undoubtedly ameliorate some of the difficulties associated with the poll tax, it would also continue to give tremendously increased power to the DES, a prospect guaranteed to frighten the libertarian right and, not least, members of the current Conservative government. On the other hand, grant-maintained status seems to exemplify what is at the heart of contemporary Conservative ideology: schools operating in the open market (thus satisfying the liberal tendency), while the central state ensures the reproduction of a stratified society. Whatever the Secretary of State might say about safeguarding the character (comprehensive or otherwise) of any opted-out school, it is highly probable that covert selection will become established. The fact that the Secretary of State makes the final decision regarding the award of grant-maintained status ensures that stratification in educational provision can be reinforced by a government which believes in its legitimacy. Given the hostility of the current administration to any form of egalitarianism there is every possibility of a return to a nation-wide selective secondary school system – but without the intrusion of local authorities. Local management of schools, in this view, is merely a stepping-stone to an entirely consumerist education system, shaped only by the considerations of ideological monopoly as maintained through the National Curriculum.

However, for the foreseeable future, most schools will remain within the local authority sector. With charge-capped, mainly urban LEAs finding it almost impossible to provide the funds for large-scale, much needed school capital expenditure, governing bodies have become increasingly fearful with regard to their duties under LMS. In this respect, the plight of the poorer inner

London boroughs, such as Hackney, is examined in some detail in Chapter 6. But, perhaps, the situation of Westbury Park Primary School in Bristol puts this into perspective. Here, the governors were reported to have refused to take on responsibility for the school's budget (Fisher, 1990, p. 20). Despite being a 'middle-class, oversubscribed school' it was housed in 'a poor building on a cramped site'.

Any attempt by governors to ameliorate these conditions would be at the expense of fewer curriculum resources for the children and would therefore affect the implementation of the National Curriculum. The only solution was to refuse to set a budget – albeit a potentially illegal act. This kind of direct action was not envisaged by the legislators when assessing potential opposition to the Education Reform Act. Perhaps this is an isolated case of an obdurate governing body. On the other hand, given that it must now more fully represent the 'consumers' of education, it would be difficult to characterize the actions of these governors as the crazed behaviour of the 'loony left'.

This chapter has sought to demonstrate not only some of the internal contradictions of LMS but also some of the wider conflicts associated with this aspect of the 1988 Act. This, however, is not to condemn the idea of increased autonomy for individual schools as such. Neither is it to suggest that all schools will fare badly under LMS; on the contrary, some will do very well indeed and find they have increased funds. But, neither can LMS be taken at face value, for its underlying message is: schools must operate in the real world and not be cosseted by the state. If schools want increased resources then they must earn the means to acquire them through taking in more pupils, as well as becoming more involved in 'enterprising' activities. They may also have to make unpopular decisions such as sacking teachers and it is already clear that LMS has led to significant job losses (see Blackburne, 1990; Nash, 1990).

REFERENCES

• Bates, S. (1990) School heads attack lack of resources. *The Guardian*, 31 March.
• Blackburne, L. (1990) Anger over LMS job losses. *Times Educational Supplement*, 25 May.

• Bristol Polytechnic Education Study Group (1989) Restructuring the education system. In Bash, L. and Coulby, D. *The Educational Reform Act: Competition and Control*. London: Cassell.

• Castle, M. (1990) Pressure from a cap that is much too tight. *Times Educational Supplement*, 18 May.

• Christchurch C. of E. Primary School, Bradford-on-Avon, Wiltshire (1990) *Newsletter to Parents*, Spring term.

• Clayton, J. (1990) Letter. *Times Educational Supplement*, 6 April, p. 19.

• Combes, A. (1990) The secrets of success. *Times Educational Supplement*, 6 April, p. 20.

• Dean, C. (1990) Abolish 'remote' county councils. *Times Educational Supplement*, 24 August, p. 2.

• DES (1988) *Local Management of Schools: A Report to the Department of Education and Science by Coopers & Lybrand*. London: DES.

• DES (1990) *ERA, a Bulletin for Schoolteachers and Governors*. Spring Issue 5. London: DES.

• Fisher, B. (1990) Alone and living dangerously. *Times Educational Supplement*, 6 July, p. 20.

• Kent County Council (1990) *Kent Governor Support Programme*. Unit 4.

• Messor, J. (1990) Primary school headteacher. Interview, March.

• Nash, I. (1990) Drastic LMS job cuts confirmed by councils. *Times Educational Supplement*, 1 June.

• Porter, J. R. (1990) Secondary school headteacher. Interview, August.

• Pyke, N. (1990) Libraries fear end is due under LMS. *Times Educational Supplement*, 24 August, p. 5.

• Roberts, B. and Ritchie, H. (1990) Management structures in secondary schools. *Educational Management and Administration* 18(3).

• Thompson, Q. (1990) Is LMS still on track? *Times Educational Supplement*, 6 July, p. 14.

• Vaughan, C. (1990) Unbalanced laughter. *The Guardian*, 27 March, p. 27.

• Wiltshire County Council (1990) Letter to headteachers.

• Wragg, E. (1990) *Times Educational Supplement*, 22 June.

6

Baker's Dozen? Education in Inner London

Crispin Jones

On April Fool's Day, 1990, the Inner London Education Authority (ILEA) ceased to exist and thirteen new local education authorities (LEAs) took its place. A day or so later, on 4 April, some of the poorest of the new authorities, all Labour controlled, were poll tax–capped by central government, potentially forcing on them draconian budget cuts. In those circumstances, the number thirteen seemed appropriate. However, with the ILEA abolished and unlikely to be replaced in its former shape, this chapter will attempt to look to the future rather than lament, or indeed praise, its passing.

The new LEAs and their 1990 political control are as follows: Camden (Labour); City of London (City of London Corporation control); Greenwich (Labour); Hackney (Labour); Hammersmith and Fulham (Labour); Islington (Labour); Lambeth (Labour); Kensington and Chelsea (Conservative); Lewisham (Labour); Southwark (Labour); Tower Hamlets (Liberal); Wandsworth (Conservative); Westminster (Conservative).

What are likely to be the main concerns and elements of education in inner London over the next decade? The short answer is that we do not really know. Thus, of necessity, this chapter will be rather short, speculative rather than definitive, indicative rather than fallaciously comprehensive. It will attempt to outline some of the educational issues that the new LEAs will have to face in the immediate period after the abolition of the ILEA and indicate some of the measures that they are adopting in order to attempt to meet these issues in a satisfactory manner. In particular the three issues of resources, teacher shortages, and the new administrations themselves will be examined.

Such a tentative response to foreseeing the future of education in inner London is not one shared by Kenneth Baker, the former

Secretary of State for Education and Science, who had been responsible, through the 1988 Education Act, for the abolition of the ILEA. On the eve of its abolition he wrote a celebratory article entitled 'A bright new term for London's children' in London's evening newspaper, the *Evening Standard* (Baker, 1990). In it, he proclaimed the benefits that were already accruing to certain parts of inner London as a result of the abolition of the ILEA, and castigated the abolished body for its financial and educational incompetence. By this time, of course, Mr Baker was no longer Secretary of State, his new role being chair of the Conservative Party, and so the article in question should perhaps be seen more as a piece of party polemic than the reasoned argument of a government minister. However, it is not unreasonable to suggest that it is a truthful reflection of the intellectual understanding that underpinned his wish, when Secretary of State, to abolish the ILEA.

In the article, he refers to the ILEA, the only directly elected LEA in Britain, as an authority that was

> remote and answered to no one. It was not responsible to London's parents, to London's teachers or to London's children. (Baker, 1990)

More, he claims it was ineffective, spending too much for too little return,

> ILEA also spent far more money per pupil than any other authority in the country, yet it presided over some of the worst exam results to be found anywhere. (Baker, 1990)

He compared such results unfavourably with other parts of London such as Barnet, 'just up the road from ILEA', an affluent, leafy suburban borough which is as comparable to much of ILEA as chalk is to cheese. Perhaps more to his point, he compared ILEA's spending to that of Liverpool: an area, he claimed, that faced equal difficulties in providing education. Here, perhaps, he was on sounder ground, for there is little doubt that in comparison with other disadvantaged inner city areas, ILEA did spend more money with little easily demonstrable return. Of course, the problem with statements like these is that the comparisons are very difficult to make, and the London 'effect', the sheer scale of the social and educational issues involved, is likely to turn a quantitative difference into a qualitative one.

Certainly, prior to the passing of the Act, few teachers in the schools of disadvantaged parts of inner London felt that they were being pampered by an over-indulgent education authority.

However, what Mr Baker's foray into journalism really reveals, apart from a wish to puff the prospects of boroughs like Wandsworth and Westminster in the local elections that were shortly to take place, is that he, no doubt along with many others in the Conservative Party, saw the ILEA as not just an inefficient and corrupt left-wing bureaucracy, but also as a real threat to much that was important in English educational life. As was argued in an earlier piece on the ILEA's abolition (Jones, 1989), a real worry about the ILEA, apart from its general oppositional and radical left-wing political stance, was its espousal of equal opportunity issues, particularly multicultural, anti-racist education. As Baker complains,

> The Authority employed three times as many inspectors to monitor its equal opportunity and anti-racist policies as it did inspectors to monitor a subject as fundamental and important as English. What utter nonsense.
>
> So we served notice on ILEA. But what was extraordinary was that the Authority refused to take any notice. (Baker, 1990)

The confusion about the nature of the ILEA inspectorate's work is matched only by the petulance at being ignored. As was argued in Chapter 2, there are elements of nationalism and racism beneath the surface of the 1988 Act, and this attack on the ILEA seems partly to support that view by suggesting that the Authority was paying too much attention to the education of black children and young black people.

So what has happened and what is likely to happen over the next few years as the new LEAs start to tackle the problems of education in the inner city of London? The first obvious factor that emerges is that the social conditions in which many pupils live are likely to remain poor. Poor-quality housing, both local authority and private, poor jobs or no jobs, and a deteriorating standard of public services, including education, are likely to continue.

To illustrate briefly the scale of this problem, it is helpful to examine the situation in one of the new LEAs, Tower Hamlets (data taken from London Borough of Tower Hamlets, 1988).

Situated immediately to the east of the City of London, Tower Hamlets has for hundreds of years been a centre for in-migration into London. The two recent main groups have been the Jews (from the 1880s to the 1930s), and the Bangladeshis (from the 1970s to the present day). As a place of in-migration to the city, Tower Hamlets, like the East End of London generally, has traditionally been poor, disregarded by central government and often the focus for xenophobic sentiments in the majority population. The anti-semitism against the Jewish population is still remembered and the racism against the current Bangladeshi population is a constant feature of life in the borough.

Because it is a borough with a strong in-migrant presence, its population continues to grow at a time when many other London boroughs' populations are declining. Thus, between 1981 and 1987, the population of Tower Hamlets grew by 9.5 per cent, while the population of Greater London fell by 0.5 per cent (London Borough of Tower Hamlets, 1988, pp. 4–5). The most obvious consequence of this for education is that there are not enough places in the schools for the children. Indeed, many hundreds of Bangladeshi children have continued to be out of school because of the inability of the ILEA and the new LEA of Tower Hamlets to provide places for them. Whether this situation would have continued for so long had the children concerned not been black is a question which remains to be answered.

Couple this shortage of school places with the high levels of poverty found in the borough and there is a recipe for a demanding educational task. Half of the population lives below the poverty line, with 19 per cent of households in 1985 having a gross income of under £2,600. Furthermore, although unemployment is slowly declining in the borough, it remains, at 17.4 per cent, the highest in Greater London (London Borough of Tower Hamlets, 1988, pp. 5–6).

Housing is similarly an area of extreme and concentrated difficulty. Despite changes in housing policy at the national level that have encouraged the sale of council properties, 48,000 of the total housing stock of some 62,000 dwellings remain in council hands (London Borough of Tower Hamlets, 1988). There are over 10,000 people on the housing waiting list, with little hope of being housed and the borough has been investigated by the Commission for Racial Equality for practising discrimination in their housing allocation policies. This accusation was upheld by the Commission after a detailed investigation (Commission for Racial Equality, 1988). It is ironic that within the borough boundary lies part of the London Docklands Development Corporation, a thriving economic area that appears to have brought little new employment or readily available housing to the borough.

With such a socio-economic background, concentrations of poverty and disadvantage present particular difficulties for inner London schools. The ILEA's own educational priority area (EPA) indicators for 1987 confirm this. Tower Hamlets came out as being the most disadvantaged area in inner London in terms of the number of children having free school meals, coming from large families, and coming from homes where the wage earners were unemployed. However – and this indicates the influence that the Bangladeshi population has on such figures – there were fewer children in care and from single parent families than anywhere else in inner London (ILEA, 1988).

A further and obvious educational issue relates to these factors: namely multilingualism in education. With over half the school population in Tower Hamlets having a home language other than English, the schools are under immense resource pressure to provide adequate language teaching, despite the funding of some 300 extra teachers by the Home Office under the Section 11 provision. However, in common with most of the other inner London boroughs, the needs of bilingual pupils have been, and are likely to continue to be, inadequately met owing to an unfortunate mix of inadequate resourcing, poor planning and a lack of educational and political determination to get the matter sorted out.

It is important to realize that this sort of educational context is not restricted to Tower Hamlets. Indeed it is replicated, in some form or another, in most of the other new LEAs. A *Times Educational Supplement* report on the prospects of the new Southwark LEA in the spring of 1990 commented:

> As a sample of the difficulties the new authority faces: nearly one in five households has a weekly income of £50 or less; 35,000 people are dependent on social security; at least 20% of all males are unemployed (45% if they are black); the number of households becoming homeless

has tripled since 1987. Over half the children are eligible
for free school meals. (St John-Brooks and Pyke, 1990, p. 11)

The educational consequences of such levels of social disadvantage are immense. The difficulties which face schools in inner
London are those common to other inner city areas but on a much
larger scale. The 1988 Education Act, as the major piece of educational legislation to be introduced for nearly half a century, might
have been expected to address these problems. The extent to
which it intervened to improve these difficulties, to ignore them,
or actually to exacerbate them, is now considered.

Compared to the state of affairs under ILEA, a major new
element introduced by the Act which is going to affect the
quality of provision is differential resourcing. ILEA redistributed
resources from the richer parts of inner London, such as the City,
Westminster, Kensington and Chelsea to poorer areas like
Southwark and Tower Hamlets. This has now stopped, apart
from any short-term contributions that might be culled from
the poll tax safety net. However, the City of London LEA, with
its financial responsibility for one school and 100 or so pupils,
appears to have something of a conscience about this, and,
amongst other things, has taken over the careers service for
the whole of London, including the outer London boroughs.

Despite such respites, the lessening of the financial load
for some has led to a greater load for the poorer boroughs.
Central government might dispute this, claiming that it is financial irresponsibility that is being curtailed. However, the feeling
of a financial stranglehold in some of the poorer boroughs has
not been helped by poll tax–capping, which has forced major
cuts in services on the new authorities almost before they have
started taking responsibility for education. The poll tax itself
brought about an inequitable financial burden on boroughs such
as Greenwich and Tower Hamlets which have high numbers of
school-age children in proportion to the adult poll tax payers.
Moreover, although there is some transitional relief being given
to the inner London boroughs by central government to soften
the financial blow of ILEA's abolition, it is generally considered
inadequate, particularly in the boroughs whose finances are
affected adversely by the change. For example, in Camden, the
ILEA budget at abolition was £64.7 million. The DES estimate
for 1990/1 was £52.77 million, which with short-term transitional

relief of £6.78 million, still leaves a gap of some £5 million (London Borough of Camden, 1990). After five years, the transitional element disappears and the true nature of the financial shortfall will be only too clear.

In contrast, the more prosperous boroughs have money to spare, with ex-ILEA administrative staff not quite believing the sums that are potentially available. Westminster, for example, is spending 58 per cent more on its schools than is estimated as sufficient by the DES. And, selling off public cemeteries apart, this is a borough generally praised for its sensible financial management by central government. The effect of the implementation of the 1988 Education Act, taken alongside the parallel legislation on the poll tax (see Chapter 1), has been to decrease the amount of money available for the education of children and young people in those areas of inner London which have the high concentrations of social and economic disadvantage. In a few richer areas more educational money has been made available.

Taken with the poll tax, this aspect of the 1988 Act may be seen as an attack on the education of some of the most disadvantaged children and young people in England and Wales. In terms of the wider themes of this book, this educational impoverishment represents one of the more visible manifestations of that class contradiction mentioned in the opening chapter. Local governments in many of the boroughs, like the ILEA before them, find themselves as the defenders of working-class educational entitlements. The conflict with central government, having been once resolved by the 1988 Act in favour of the DES, is still likely to continue. The issue of resources is likely to be the important component of this conflict. Whether the boroughs also find themselves in ideological conflict with central government over issues such as equal opportunities policies remains to be seen. Were this to be the case, being small and divided they might not be seen to manifest such a strong challenge as the disbanded ILEA.

Differential resourcing has an enormous impact upon another area, without which the educational service ceases to exist, namely teacher supply. This is because the financial problems facing many of the new LEAs have exacerbated the already existing difficulty of teacher supply. Inner London's schools, as is well known, currently have a chronic shortage of teachers, particularly at the primary level. As the resource shortages become more acute and more public, this situation is almost certain to get worse. Yet whatever the hopes and aspirations of the new LEAs, without teachers nothing of any great import will be achieved.

The break-up of the ILEA and the introduction of the radical series of measures consequent upon the passing of the 1988 Education Act exacerbated the pressures upon teachers in schools in inner London. Figures released by the DES in the Autumn of 1989 suggest a long-term improvement in teacher supply while noting current shortages in the south-east of England most notably in Kent, Essex and Greater London. Moreover, according to the DES, at that time only two LEAs – Waltham Forest and the ILEA – admitted to being extremely concerned. Further evidence of the problem in the inner London area was given in the survey carried out by the National Association of Head Teachers (NAHT), released at almost the same time as the DES figures, indicating, among other things, that there was wide variation *within* the 28 per cent annual resignation rate of the ILEA and that some 40 per cent of the resigning teachers were leaving teaching altogether. More, the figures for Tower Hamlets and Southwark for example, indicate that these particular parts of the ILEA are at the worse end of that variation (Coulby and Jones, 1990).

Yet, with Tower Hamlets and Southwark being new LEAs with all the difficulties that implies, the difficulty of teacher recruitment and retention is a major issue which potentially jeopardizes all that they are attempting to provide. Moreover, although there is little disagreement about national and LEA statistics on teacher numbers, there is widespread dispute about causes and future trends. Furthermore, there is the most disturbing point that when schools fail to retain their teachers, those leaving are increasingly leaving the teaching profession altogether rather than moving to another school and/or LEA. Thus schools that fail to retain their staff threaten not only themselves and their LEA, but the service as a whole. More bluntly, if the new London LEAs fail to retain their teachers they are likely to lose these teachers for the whole of the teaching service.

How have the new LEAs responded to this issue? The answer is mainly through the short-sighted provision of benefits packages. The provision of some form of housing support for beginning teachers is an important way of attracting people to the capital. Beyond this, the effectiveness of benefit packages is open to question. Such policies need more careful evaluation than they are being given at present, particularly as they use scarce resources and are of unproven value. Indeed, 'package competition' between the new LEAs may, in the medium to long term, be counter-productive.

If working in the inner city is to be made more attractive to young teachers, it is the implementation of the in-post elements of such packages, particularly in relation to induction, support and INSET, that need close examination, as failure in this area will affect retention and ultimately, recruitment itself. As yet, there is little indication of these and related issues being given the attention that they deserve and need by the new LEAs. To be fair, however, the supply of sufficient numbers of well-qualified and well-motivated teachers is an issue beyond the control of individual LEAs. The nationally determined salary levels of teachers and the status they are publicly seen to hold are also issues that need to be addressed. These issues are taken up in the final chapter. Until teachers obtain appropriate financial and status recognition, staff shortages in many inner London schools are likely to persist.

Assuming for the moment, however, that the new LEAs will have sufficient teachers, what will these teachers do? Some guidance is given by the individual educational development plans that were drawn up by each of the new LEAs. These documents make fascinating reading and are an illuminating snapshot of urban educational concerns in London in the late 1980s. Each of the boroughs was required, by the 1988 Education Act, to produce an educational development plan for the new LEA, these plans having to be approved by the Secretary of State. The plans demonstrate an interesting variety of responses to many similar educational issues. However, when reading the development plans, there is little sense of the issues raised by teacher shortages and generally inadequate financing. In a sense, this is understandable, as the plans represent an ideal system rather than the reality with which the boroughs were soon to be faced. This is true of many aspects of the development plans, not merely those parts devoted to resource issues. What most of the plans did do, however, was to portray an accurate account of the socio-economic circumstances within which they had to prepare a new educational administration.

Within that useful context-setting exercise, the development plans already appear somewhat dated documents, overtaken by the swift pace of events that have followed on the abolition of the ILEA. An examination of them reveals a huge variation of potential policies. Although perhaps genuine in intent, many of the new ideas that were being proposed, from left- and right-wing councils alike, were in practice mainly presentational. This was because all the new LEAs were inheriting a school system which could not be easily changed, as, for instance, the new Director of Education for Wandsworth, Donald Naismith, quickly found out. His initial attempts to introduce a magnet school system were firmly rebuffed by the Wandsworth secondary heads and it is still unclear as to how effective he can be in introducing the series of radical changes he sees as necessary to rejuvenate secondary education in the borough.

An initially unexpected aspect of abolition was the enthusiasm that Labour, Liberal and Conservative councils all quickly revealed in relation to running their own education system. This new enthusiasm may reveal just how much power local councillors have lost in other fields in recent years. As councillors get to grips with the task of running an education system, the clarification of roles between officers and members is likely to prove to be quite a turbulent process. Despite such initial difficulties, it is probable that there is a real enthusiasm amongst members for making education 'work' in the boroughs, and this will, in the main, prove beneficial.

A further dimension to the boroughs' enthusiasm for control of education is the comparative lack of commitment by many of them to maintaining those cross-authority services that ILEA provided but which no single one of the new LEAs has the resources to maintain by itself. A good example of such a service was the ILEA's unit that looked after the education of Travellers' children on a cross-London basis, members of the unit often following the children as they moved around the ILEA. During the negotiations over the future of this unit, it was agreed that the new Southwark LEA would host the unit and that other new LEAs would buy in its services, thus avoiding wasteful duplication, or, more likely, no provision at all. However, as Richard Edwards, an assistant director in Southwark, publicly commented:

Now we have a situation where a team could be working with

a travelling family for some time, then be unable to continue if the family moved somewhere like Tower Hamlets, which has not subscribed to the service. The Government thought that after lead boroughs were agreed, others would be happy to contribute. That simply isn't happening. (quoted in Braid, 1990, p. 4)

Similar reluctances over other services are beginning to emerge, no doubt fuelled by the desperate need for some of the new LEAs to make major cuts in services as a result of poll tax–capping.

Another aspect of difficulties over cross-borough services had to be resolved by the courts. This was in relation to the provision of school places to out-of-borough children. Greenwich LEA wished to give priority to its own borough's children over children from other boroughs. A secondary school that was very popular with middle-class parents was close to the border of neighbouring Lewisham and had traditionally taken children from this other borough, never an issue within the ILEA. When Greenwich put up a policy which would have denied places to many of the Lewisham parents, Greenwich was taken to court and lost. The implications of this judgment for other LEAs are momentous, and, although leave to appeal was refused, the judgment is bound to cause problems in the future, particularly in relation to LEA planning.

The likely diminution of cross-borough cooperation is to be regretted but it does not bulk large in the eyes of those running the new LEAs. Furthermore, staffing and financial problems apart – and it is very difficult, except theoretically, to put such major problems on one side – the new LEAs are also having to deal with the issues that are demoralizing their colleagues up and down the country, namely the introduction of the new National Curriculum, the impending chaos of local management of schools (LMS), open enrolment, and the other major changes consequent upon the implementation of the 1988 Education Act (all described and analysed in previous chapters). It is true that the new LEAs have been granted a breathing space in relation to LMS, but it has quickly become clear that the financial problems that surround some of them will be made worse by its implementation. Other chapters in this book have pointed to the ways in which some sections of the 1988 Act are in contradiction and conflict with each other. For the inner London boroughs the difficulty presented by the Act is that everything has to happen at once. They have not only been given the massive job of educating some of the nation's most disadvantaged children and young people in succession to the ILEA, but this task has also been given to them at a time of maximum change and uncertainty in the education system. For schools in inner London, their control, financing, management, curriculum and assessment are all meant to change at the same time.

However, although the ILEA has gone, and despite the major changes brought about by the Act, the new LEAs are dealing with the same schools, the same type of children, and many of the same teachers as did the previous authority. In other words there is a danger of assuming that the chaos of transition is likely to be a permanent feature of educational life in inner London. But there are positive things happening in the new LEAs. One of the potentially most exciting is the possibility of greater local accountability. As Peter Mitchell, the new Director of Education for Camden, noted,

> One of the clear intentions of the Education Reform Act is to see that resources for education are managed by those who have direct links with the students, whether they be children, adolescents or adults. Parents and governors will thus be much more involved in working with headteachers and teachers. As a new LEA we must, therefore, work in partnership with these groups. We will share a common concern with seeing that resources are used in the best interests of students. (Mitchell, 1990, p. 1)

This can all too easily be read as rhetoric but it should rather be seen in the context of one of the three major priorities of this new LEA, namely, 'monitoring and evaluating the quality of education provided for students of all ages in Camden' (Mitchell, 1990, p. 1). What comments like this also reveal is a fresh enthusiasm amongst the new officers and members. As Alan Wood, a Camden councillor, puts it,

> Whilst we rightfully and gratefully acknowledge the achievements of the ILEA we now need to implement fresh thinking and ideas. (London Borough of Camden, 1990, p. 4)

This comment suggests the widely held view that however good the ILEA was, more could be done by new, enthusiastic and smaller LEAs.

It is still too early to tell on this, initial teething problems tending to obscure such progress as is being made. An example of this is that many teachers who worked for the old ILEA are still not happy with their new LEAs. The almost-to-be-expected initial hiccups notwithstanding (such as those over pay), there was a widespread feeling that if the old ILEA felt distant and out of touch with schools, many of the new LEAs were equally out of touch, their comparative smallness providing neither intimacy nor competence and often the reverse. An initial analysis of such feelings of malaise indicates that they seem to fall into three categories. Firstly, there is a disenchantment with certain aspects of the management styles of the new LEAs. Secondly, there is a more general disillusion engendered by the increasing impact on the same schools and colleges of the range of measures outlined in the 1988 Education Act. The third factor is that schools and colleges are, like the new LEAs, also flexing their muscles, supported by those aspects of the Act that delegate more power to individual institutions. Thus there are greater than normal and increasing tensions within schools as well as between them and their new LEAs. Conflicts over policy or resources at school level form part of the background to difficulties over teacher recruitment. Conflict between schools and the new boroughs is likely to be manifested through attempts to opt out. There is an interesting small-scale contradiction in the 1988 Act here. Radical schools, teachers and parents who find themselves, through the dismemberment of the ILEA, in Conservative LEA control, may be able to escape it by using another component of the Act to become grant-maintained schools.

Another element of disenchantment, and one not really related to ILEA's abolition, is that teachers in many schools do feel somewhat beleaguered owing to the continued adverse media coverage of education and to the fact that many of their colleagues are leaving or seeking to leave whilst their replacements have yet to appear. Thus, as the new school year 1990/1 began, it started in inner London with many children yet again being sent home because there were no teachers to teach them. This was, of course, not new, but there was increasing concern being expressed by experienced teachers working within already difficult schools about the effect of such interrupted schooling on the children's attitude to learning.

It is important to put these adverse feelings alongside the more optimistic perspectives held by many in the administrative structures of the new LEAs. In a curious sense, both perspectives are accurate. This is because, although there are considerable difficulties facing the new LEAs, the fundamental issues remain the same in inner London's schools. Certainly, the schooling system continues to fail working-class children in large numbers, but educational standards in the ILEA were slowly rising and will probably continue to do so in many of the new LEAs. Major initiatives undertaken by the ILEA, such as the London Record of Achievement, its pioneering Compact scheme, its anti-racist and anti-sexist policies, its ambitious induction and INSET programmes, show what can be done in adverse circumstances. The new LEAs, in other words, have a firm base of achievement and a commitment to excellence and equality which may see them through their initial starting-up difficulties.

This optimism will only be substantiated, however, if the financial constraints and teacher shortages, issues over which the new LEAs have little control, are alleviated and positive steps taken to assert and demonstrate the value of education to the community. In other words, the Conservative central government, having settled its scores with the ILEA, should not continue that vendetta with the succeeding LEAs. The new boroughs' commitment is clear; as the Hammersmith and Fulham Development Plan put it:

> Good quality education is therefore for our common benefit, and not just a means of achieving advancement or fulfilment in individuals. In 1944, there was widespread recognition in this country of the significance of education for a coherent, stable, just and free society. Over the past two decades, emphasis has shifted to economic utility, wealth creation, and individualism as being the basic forces governing education requirements.
>
> In building its education service, Hammersmith and Fulham Council believes in re-emphasising some of these earlier basic principles of collective vision and purpose. We see education as something through which all people become confident, capable, autonomous citizens, able to manage their lives with a sense of purpose and of responsibility to

others. We see it as a public good, like health and housing, to which we should all be willing to contribute. (London Borough of Hammersmith and Fulham, 1989, p. 1)

This statement of intent, and many of the other boroughs made similar ones, asserts that education in inner London is no longer about whether or not the ILEA should have been abolished. It is about whether British society as a whole, working through the new inner London LEAs, really does have a commitment to providing the resources needed to ensure that all London's children are provided with the education of quality which it is their right to expect. The challenge has been set.

REFERENCES

• Baker, K. (1990) A bright new term for London's children. *Evening Standard*, 30 March, p. 7.
• Braid, M. (1990) Successor to ILEA 'failing to cooperate'. *The Independent*, 21 August, p. 4.
• Commission for Racial Equality (1988) *Housing and Discrimination: Report of a Formal Investigation into the London Borough of Tower Hamlets*. London: CRE.
• Coulby, D. and Jones, C. (1990) Teacher retention in urban primary schools. Unpublished paper.
• ILEA (1988) *Deprivation Indices 1987*. London: ILEA Research and Statistics Branch.
• Jones, C. (1989) The abolition of the ILEA. In Bash, L. and Coulby, D. *The Education Reform Act: Competition and Control*. London: Cassell.
• London Borough of Camden (1990) *Camden Education News* 1, February 1990.
• London Borough of Hammersmith and Fulham (1989) *Education in 1990: Getting It Right*. London: London Borough of Hammersmith and Fulham.
• London Borough of Tower Hamlets (1988) *Getting It Right: Draft Development Plan*. London: London Borough of Tower Hamlets.
• Mitchell, P. (1990) The new Education Department. *Camden Education News* 1, February.
• St John-Brooks, C. and Pyke, N. (1990) The New LEAs. *Times Educational Supplement*, 6 April, p. 11.

7
Beyond Compulsory Schooling

Leslie Bash

INTRODUCTION

Previous chapters in this book have concentrated on the practical effects of the 1988 Act in relation to the compulsory years of schooling. Correctly, the National Curriculum, assessment and testing, and the governance of schools have been viewed as the core of the legislation. Yet, at the same time, the 1988 Act has had a profound affect upon the provision of education and training beyond the statutory school-leaving age. While the most obvious consequences have been for the governance and financing of higher education, the direct impact upon the further education and vocational training sectors has been immense. Criticism of the state of further and higher education has not been confined to the left of the political spectrum – indeed, many of the more strident comments have been from employers who have understood the need for a more highly educated population of young people as the basis for a sound, competitive economy. Yet, the curious mixture of elitism and *ad hoc* policy-making, characteristic of British governments since the last century, has continued to result in a wastage of human resources and a workforce ill-suited to current, let alone future, economic demands.

The ideology of competition, as reinforced by the Education Reform Act, has had the consequence of reaffirming the hierarchical structure of post-compulsory education. The 16 to 19 provision is still largely divided along academic/vocational lines and in this respect maintained colleges of further education retain an inferior status. At the same time, schools with sixth forms compete to attract the customers in a bid to attract more LMS funding (see Chapter 5), or to prevent closure, or to opt out of local authority control. Elsewhere, in the higher education sector,

121

the creation of quasi-independent 'corporations' and the establishment of the two funding bodies – the Universities Funding Council (UFC) and the Polytechnics and Colleges Funding Council (PCFC) – has resulted in frenetic activity.

It will be argued in this chapter that the continuing stratified structure of post-compulsory education has been reinforced by the 1988 Act. Moreover, the nationalization of public sector higher education, the tighter grip over university resourcing, and the introduction of competitive funding has centralized educational decision-making to the extent that there is some degree of conflict with residual elements of liberal ideology. It is ironic that much that is done in the name of free market economics not only conflicts with the ideas of those classical economists (such as Adam Smith) who have been canonized by right-wing politicians, but also encourages inefficiency and wastefulness – the very opposite of what was apparently intended. It is arguable that the government's understanding of the dynamics of post-compulsory education was so poor that it was willing to sacrifice its own professed goal of an economically powerful Britain to an anachronistic *laissez-faire* ideology.

Yet, at first glance, the Education Reform Act has gone some way towards making coherent much of post-compulsory education. This is something of an achievement in an area fraught with confusion of terminology and constituting a multitude of provision. From the days of the Mechanics Institutes and the confinement of university places to the exceptionally privileged, through to the Business and Technician Education Council (BTEC), youth training and polytechnics, there has been little in the way of comprehensive direction from the central state.

Here, the 1988 Act has undoubtedly instituted significant change, although there had been a number of central state initiatives in relation to the 16 to 19 age group during the 1970s and 1980s. Such initiatives, however, mainly resulted from panic over youth unemployment and Britain's general economic situation rather than from any carefully constructed policy regarding 16 to 19 education and training. Nor was there a fundamental difference in the approach of the last Labour government (which brought in the Youth Opportunities Programme (YOP) in 1978, offering a period of work experience and training in 'social and life skills' to the young unemployed) and that of the first Thatcher administration. However, the latter was rather more keen to take the opportunity to begin a shift in the control of education and, at the same time, to demonstrate that youth unemployment was essentially the fault of young people themselves. This illustrated two of the major, if sometimes conflicting, aspects of modern Conservative ideology: an emphasis upon individuals and their responsibilities, and the importance of centralized social control.

The shift in the control of education took shape in the ascendancy of the Manpower Services Commission (MSC), an organization with a close relationship with the Department of Employment, but which had a semi-autonomous existence with representatives from government, employers and trades unions involved in its running (a well-known example of a quango). It was under the first Thatcher government that the Youth Training Scheme (YTS) was introduced in 1982 by the MSC. While sceptics were no more impressed by YTS than by YOP, seeing it as yet another reactive response to youth unemployment, it did apparently offer a new approach to the vocational training of young people, allied as it was to ideas of flexibility and transferable skills in an ever-changing technological and economic world. Once YTS became established the government decided that there was little to stop it from penetrating the secondary school curriculum in order to demonstrate the poverty of much of the content of 14 to 18 education for the average pupil. Consequently, under the auspices of the MSC, the Technical and Vocational Education Initiative (TVEI) was launched as a programme, constructed on a local consortium basis, to give some kind of work orientation to what pupils were doing at the upper secondary school level. With hindsight, what appeared to be a struggle for power and influence over the control of education and training between two arms of central government – the Department of Employment (via the MSC) and the DES – was, in fact, the first battle in the war against the local education authorities. Once the DES was shown to be impotent in the face of both the LEAs and the Department of Employment it was clearly time to assert its authority and, indeed, expand its role through new legislation. It is, perhaps, for future historians and former cabinet ministers to confirm whether this was the Conservative master plan, but it is enough to recognize the smooth progression of events from 1979 to 1990.

As a result, it was relatively easy for the Conservatives, after having gained power in 1979, to ensure that the MSC became the mouthpiece for central government through the gradual easing-out of trade union representatives and anyone else who might provide an alternative to the dominant view. In the final event, the MSC (and its successor, the Training Agency) was wound up and YTS was simply renamed Youth Training, to be governed by locally-based Training and Enterprise Councils (TECs) (see pp. 128–9). Whether, then, this was intended as the precursor to the ascendancy of the DES as a powerful central body with regard to post-compulsory education remains to be seen although it is clear that the 1988 Act, at least in principle, has taken this phase on board.

This can be seen in the language of the Act which suggests that post-16 education and training should reflect the diverse needs of society. Although not spelt out in the Act, in practice this meant that while many of the 16 to 19 age group would be expected to remain at school to pursue an A-level programme, others would enter further education colleges or youth training schemes. Further education remains in the hands of local authorities, having been largely separated from public sector higher education (polytechnics and major colleges of higher education), which is now centrally funded. On the other hand, the governing bodies of FE colleges received a considerable degree of autonomy through the delegation of financial and other managerial powers, i.e. the establishment of the local management of further education. At the same time, these governing bodies became more representative of employers' interests through a change in their composition. Sharp (1990, p. 117) states that following the legislation, the DES, in Circular 9/88, required certain factors to be taken into account by LEAs, in their planning for further education such as: demographic trends, labour market needs, post-16 participation rates, preferences for FE as against school, reorganization plans, and access provision.

However, in contrast to its provisions for the 5 to 16 age group, the 1988 Act remains largely silent on the content of post-16 education and training. Yet the impact of the National Curriculum and the measures on assessment and testing upon further and higher education is quite significant. In so far as the pathways taken by young people beyond the age of 16 are shaped by previous educational experiences, which must include the diversity of judgements made regarding educational achievement, this is undoubtedly true. More than this, however, is the impact of the National Curriculum and the nature of assessment procedures upon GCSE, and, subsequently, A-level, vocational, professional and degree courses. The full consequences, of course, cannot be known until these aspects of the Act work their way through the system, although it is now evident that proposals for a broader sixth form/A-level curriculum are not totally unrelated to concerns for the school curriculum as a whole. If one argument for the introduction of a national curriculum for children of compulsory school age is the importance of inculcating a common culture with a 'unity of purpose' (Bash and Coulby, 1989, p. 55) then there is every reason to support its extension to the sixth form (if not the entire 16 to 19) sector. In addition, if the rhetoric surrounding the importance of broad curriculum for the country's economic advance is to be taken seriously then there can be few arguments for the continuation of a narrow post-16 education (see pp. 137-8).

Whether this will ultimately mean a broadening of the undergraduate curriculum and, perhaps, the reintroduction of a liberal studies perspective to vocational training is another matter. While many polytechnics and colleges have undoubtedly been in the forefront of the liberalization process in undergraduate education, pioneering new kinds of degree courses which have cut across traditional academic lines, universities have remained relatively conservative in these matters. At the time of writing, it might be noted that Keele, which is alone among English universities in offering a common, broad undergraduate first year in a four-year course, does not appear to have a secure financial future (Utley, 1990). A more realistic possibility, then, is some kind of rearrangement of the higher education hierarchy which does not necessarily conform to the current binary division (see pp. 134-5). Indeed, it is more likely to reflect the stratified curriculum which, given 'overcrowdedness' and the difficulties over assessment and testing (see Chapter 3), now seems to be the practical outcome of the 1988 Act.

As for vocational training, the establishment of the National Council for Vocational Qualifications (NCVQ) might be viewed as a step in a direction opposed to the inculcation of a broad educational outlook. Accordingly, the NCVQ has an explicit remit to see that courses leading to BTEC, City and Guilds, RSA, and other certificates place an emphasis upon competency criteria

(Bash and Coulby, 1989, p. 82). More specifically, the NCVQ is supposed to:

- secure standards of occupational competence and ensure that vocational qualifications are based on these;
- design and implement a new national framework for vocational qualifications;
- approve bodies making accredited awards;
- obtain comprehensive coverage of all occupational sectors;
- secure arrangements for quality assurance;
- set up effective liaison with bodies awarding vocational qualifications;
- establish a national database for vocational qualifications;
- undertake, or arrange to be undertaken, research and development to discharge these functions;
- promote vocational education, training and qualifications. (Shackleton, 1988, p. 58)

The NCVQ remit would, from the above, appear to meet the demands of employers who have been less than satisfied with a diversity of vocational qualifications with varying degrees of relevance. Thus:

college departments will need to move away from a traditional approach based on the teaching and assessment of knowledge to an approach which also conveys practical skills with direct application on the job. (Libby and Hull, 1988, p. 11)

With a significant shift away from colleges towards the workplace, the NCVQ seems to be returning vocational education to a previous era. Just when FE was beginning to place itself in the mainstream of educational innovation, especially in such area as profiling and records of achievement, central government has decided once more to demonstrate its concern for standards. As with the emphasis upon attainment targets in the National Curriculum, so the NCVQ has adopted an approach to accreditation through task analysis. Critics have been blunt in their comments on the role of NCVQ, considering it to be in danger of ignoring the advances made in BTEC, CPVE, and even YTS, in relation to 'insights, experiences and knowledge about the world' and 'holistic training' (Prately, 1988, p. 65). Even if the National

Curriculum encourages a similar 'objectives' approach to learning, there is, at least, a breadth of subjects to be studied by the majority of children, with the addition of cross-curricular themes. Unfortunately, the tendency for a narrowing of perspectives has been endemic to vocational training, given the traditionalist views of British employers.

Where does this leave the colleges? FE has always occupied a precarious place within the English education system, with loyalties divided between students and employers. Given the increased proportion of those working in further education who have undergone initial teacher training, and the positive educational outlook of the National Association of Teachers in Further and Higher Education (NATFHE), there is bound to be some optimism. The editorial comments in the *NATFHE Journal* (May/June, 1990) accordingly suggest that education can be put back into training, as long as NCVQ is not left completely to the mercy of employers with their positive view of narrow skills training. On the other hand, this merely opens up the wider question of how 16 to 19 education and training as a whole should be structured, and, here, it is important to juxtapose diverse aspects of central government policy in order to highlight the incoherent character of this part of the system.

VOCATIONALISM VERSUS ACADEMIC EDUCATION

Accordingly, an apparent contradiction within central government policy (previously noted on pp. 25-8) has been the emphasis of the Act on a traditionalist view of the curriculum, together with a narrow approach to assessment and testing, as against the vocationalist policies expressed through the Youth Training Scheme, TVEI, CPVE, and other initiatives (Bash and Coulby, 1989, pp. 111-12). This contradiction betrays a long-standing elitist approach to education which has reflected the thinking of both the major political parties. Not only does the divisiveness perpetuated by this contradictory approach emphasize the backwardness of the British economy and associated structures, it also illustrates the poverty of imagination among many politicians. This last point is given further credence by the Conservative government's latest ideas (May 1991) regarding post-compulsory education, in which the vocational/academic divide remains firmly entrenched. Otherwise, vocationalism has continued unabated, with an overhaul of training policy and the creation of locally based TECs which will now have the responsibility of piloting training credit schemes – an initiative to encourage a greater uptake of training opportunities through the introduction of a market element.

The creation of TECs has been accompanied by the disbandment of the Training Agency. Consequently, at a time when Secretaries of State consistently looked in an envious manner at countries such as the Federal Republic of Germany which possessed centralized vocational training systems, the British government decided that a national training body was unnecessary. At the time of writing it is unclear whether the Department of Employment will retain some overall responsibility for vocational training/education policy or whether it will devolve to the National Council for Vocational Qualifications (Jackson, 1990).

Through the introduction of training credits the educational voucher scheme has at last resurfaced after having been temporarily buried by the Conservative Party, but in a form which does not immediately impact upon the education system as a whole. Instead, these vouchers will constitute a particular kind of 'truck money' redeemable only through the TEC programmes. As a result, LEAs and their FE colleges will again become marginalized as TECs, like the MSC before them, allow employers to dictate narrow training needs (*NATFHE Journal*, March/April, 1990). Indeed, the immediate conflict with the stated aims of the Education Reform Act in connection with further education is absolutely clear, for as the *NATFHE Journal* editorial asks:

> Whatever happened to LEA planning, formula-funding and the enhanced powers of FE governing bodies, the cornerstones of the 1988 Act? (*NATFHE Journal*, March/April, 1990, p. 3)

Once more, it would seem that the role of LEAs is further diminished, but this time as a result of central government setting up – and funding – alternative *local* bodies. No doubt, TECs will seek the legitimacy formerly accorded to local authorities – especially those which are now dubbed high spenders. In this way, the accusation that control of vocational training was in the hands of civil servants (as it apparently was under the MSC) can no longer be levelled at the government. On the contrary, TECs will reflect the needs of locally based employers, and by implication, the needs of present and future employees in the community.

There is not much that has been mentioned so far which would suggest that there has been a fundamental change in the segregated nature of post-compulsory education and training. Indeed, the divided system remains essentially unchallenged and the Act provides further support for an elitist approach in its impact on such moves as there had been to reorganize 16 to 19 education and training along comprehensive lines.

BRAKE ON TERTIARY REORGANIZATION

With the elevation of the comprehensive debate to the post-compulsory sector of education, the impact of the 1988 Act has been quite marked, especially in relation to the structure of 16 to 19 education and training. It is here that some of the most fundamental contradictions in policy have manifested themselves. The break-up of the Inner London Education Authority and the fiscal squeeze imposed upon local authorities by the imposition of the poll tax (and poll tax–capping) have resulted in all-out struggles by educational institutions to maintain their share of the market. This comes in the midst of a demographic dip with increasingly fewer members of this age group available as customers.

As a result, managers of schools with sixth forms, sixth-form colleges and centres, as well as FE colleges, became increasingly entrepreneurial in their attempt to survive in the midst of falling rolls. This was by no means a new phenomenon: further education colleges have for some time been in the business of creating demand for their services. In recent times they have followed the pathway constructed by the former Manpower Services Commission and have sought to provide education and training allegedly more orientated towards the consumer (student, parent, employer, and – arguably – the state). YTS, information technology courses, adult training, short courses for industry and the like, became increasingly important in the wake of a decline in traditional craft training.

However, the situation has moved on apace as a result of the 1988 Act. With local management, educational providers for the 16 to 19 age group have been set free and, consequently, the role of local education authorities is now more narrowly defined. Further education colleges will, as a result of the domination of their governing bodies by employers and their complete autonomy over the allocation of financial resources, have the opportunity of becoming successful business operations. Indeed, many have already set up their own college companies to provide all kinds of services (at full cost) from consultancies to tailor-made short courses. These newly 'independent' providers, now freed from imposed LEA policies and from ceilings on student numbers, will be deemed to have few excuses should they fail to satisfy consumer demand.

The prospect of many providers competing for student numbers in a declining age-cohort may be exciting for members of the Adam Smith Institute or the Institute of Economic Affairs, since the weak and inefficient will be weeded out as a consequence of a 'natural' process rather than bureaucratic edict. On the other hand, a policy of tertiary reorganization might also satisfy free market criteria such as the efficient use of resources and the enhancement of consumer choice. Yet, it may be resisted because it is perceived as a direct consequence of public planning and not as a result of the operations of the market.

The pressures to reorganize 16 to 19 education in England and Wales have undoubtedly increased in recent years and will gain momentum. Urban local education authorities, in particular, will seek further ways of minimizing the threats to their existence – from increased opting out by schools on the one hand, to the establishment of TECs on the other. In the face of falling student rolls and fiscal crisis the abandonment of school sixth forms and the establishment of tertiary colleges to provide both 'academic' and 'vocational' schooling in place of further education colleges must appear attractive.

At the same time, there are ideological as well as pragmatic considerations. Here, the case for the reorganization of 16 to 19 education in England and Wales along comprehensive, integrated lines rests upon a number of distinct premises. Prominent amongst these is the assumption of equality of opportunity and the ending of social divisions in education. While the abandonment of tripartitism at the 11 to 16 age phase is now complete in most local education authorities segregation remains at the post-compulsory level. This is not altogether surprising, since the popular expectation that the majority of young people will terminate their education and seek employment is a difficult one to counter, despite changes in work opportunities. Yet, rationally, there would appear to be a number of gains for prospective students in a tertiary set-up, not least the broadening of choice as far as courses of study are concerned. Whereas schools are rarely able to offer a complete range of A-level subjects, tertiary colleges can be found which provide the opportunity to study Greek and Latin (to satisfy traditionalists) as well as the more up-beat areas of Information Technology and minority community languages.

Although a number of Labour LEAs committed themselves to tertiary policies for these kinds of reasons (e.g. ILEA, Wolverhampton), others singularly failed to do so. This is not merely a reflection of the continuation of elitism but also of the perceived need to retain power, particularly where the votes of middle-class parents (who may not wish their children's academic education to be polluted by FE vocationalism) carry a good deal of weight.

In the era of LMS, headteachers and governors of secondary schools may fear that the loss of their sixth forms to newly established tertiary colleges not only threatens their funding but also their territories. It is not entirely accidental that the first tertiary colleges to be established (as in Exeter and Yeovil), as well as the earlier village colleges in Cambridgeshire, lay outside the metropolitan areas of England and Wales. We might conclude that the relatively homogeneous populations of these areas, together with fairly close-knit educational institutions, have encouraged policy-makers to consider tertiary reorganization, particularly in the wake of falling rolls and a declining 16 to 19 age group.

While the Inner London Education Authority, for example, had an established policy of tertiary reorganization, the pattern of secondary schooling in ILEA was still such that 'going tertiary' threatened the very existence of some schools. The proposal to abolish sixth-form provision in schools and relocate within newly established tertiary colleges clearly dealt a blow to small secondary schools as the survival of the latter becomes problematic. In the wake to LMS and opting out, headteachers, governing bodies, and parents have found themselves fighting hard to retain independence for their schools.

The difficulties faced by any local education authority in England and Wales in dealing with post-16 education are, then, considerable. A number of these difficulties deserve to be mentioned, in the wake of disruption of LEA reorganization plans as a result of successful applications for grant-maintained status by secondary schools. Secondary school rolls will continue to fall; the number staying on at school after 16 is likely to remain fairly static. It is an article of faith that reorganization will improve the participation rate, although projections suggest that they will not. Despite some increase following the 1990 GCSE results, with participation in full-time vocational as well as A-level courses, Sir Claus Moser's speech to the British Association had a significant media impact. In it, Moser lamented 'the miserable failure of the English (and to a less miserable extent, the Scottish) education systems to retain 16 to 18 year-olds in full-time education' (Maclure, 1990, p. 22).

It is self-evident that unit costs will remain high if the traditional sixth forms continue to recruit poorly (150 being the minimum size for a viable sixth form according to the recommendation of the Secretary of State). Further, while consortia arrangements can be more efficient in this respect they are expensive in terms of travel and of management. Finally, there are the difficulties of coping with the knock-on effects of the National Curriculum with the mixture of GCSE, traditional A-level courses, and a variety of work-related courses. LEAs may well have enough on their plates without also having to consider the demands of central government vocationalism and the need to build links to industry and commerce and to bridge the academic/vocational divide.

The choices for the most effective form of post-16 education are difficult enough to make in small towns or in large homogeneous cities such as Sheffield. But in a metropolitan area such as London it is especially so, and any plan which fails to reflect the complexity and plurality of values found in any city in terms of its social divisions and its spatial and residential distribution (and it is difficult to see how any plan could do justice to that complexity) will certainly turn out to be ineffective. The changing urban housing market, the present communities and neighbourhoods, the historical siting of educational establishments, the changing mosaic of ethnic groups, and the routes and variety of travel all contribute to the difficulties of meeting the educational needs of young people.

The restructuring of post-16 education in London has now been additionally complicated by the abolition of ILEA, the opting-out process and the introduction of the poll tax. The siting of schools and colleges bears no relationship whatsoever to inner London borough boundaries. On the one hand, it is estimated that some 20,000 students cross boundaries to obtain their education and, on the other, secondary schools regularly recruit from feeder primary schools across boroughs. To take one example, Pimlico School in the south of Westminster recruits from 75 feeder schools and takes 75 per cent of its total intake from outside the Borough of Westminster.

One conclusion from this examination of moves towards tertiary reorganization is that, in principle, they satisfy both efforts to democratize post-compulsory education and criteria of efficiency in provision. Yet, parental choice, both in its individualistic and collective forms, challenges both these aspects. Open enrolment will, supposedly, reflect consumer choice in action; it is just as likely, however, to reflect collective perceptions of what may be regarded as appropriate schools for children from particular backgrounds or who are categorized in a certain manner – ethnic minorities, religious communities, gender groupings, social classes, etc.

It is likely, then, that the progress of tertiary reorganization will reflect the continuing difficulties faced by local councils, whether economic, social or political. Urban education systems in particular, comprise not merely the providers on the one hand and the consumers (parents and students) on the other, but also employers, religious bodies, teachers, class and ethnic groups, and so on. The myth of consumer choice that is consistently upheld by the educational free-marketeers is shattered by the reality of those metropolitan areas characterized by social division and inequalities of political and economic power. Yet, with the emergence of the new education authorities in London, anxious to gain the confidence of the electorate in general and parents in particular, there are likely to be few hasty moves to abolish sixth-form provision in schools and establish a tertiary system lest such schools become lost to the LEA altogether.

This, of course, supposedly demonstrates to central government, yet again, the merits of the free market and the bankruptcy of bureaucratic local education authorities. The power of the consumer, so it is argued, will eventually show that there is no need for planned provision of 16 to 19 education, especially if it is along comprehensive lines, since the market will sort the situation out to everyone's satisfaction. Local authorities, as planning mechanisms, impose their will on all and sundry without taking regard of individual preferences. As such, they are seen at best as ineffective and at worst as tyrannies. Good (i.e. popular) schools with thriving sixth forms and a range of A-level and other courses will continue to attract students. Poor schools will go to the wall. Further education colleges will, however, provide the usual mix of full- and part-time work-related courses, together with a number of A-level subjects. FE colleges in particular will be responsive to the market as a result of their close connection with the fortunes of industry. More realistically, however, the result is likely to be a wastage of resources (human and otherwise) and increased educational stratification.

THE STATE OF HIGHER EDUCATION

On the surface, apart from the abolition of tenure for lecturers, the 1988 Act left the university sector untouched, except that the replacement of the Universities Grants Committee by the Universities Funding Council (UFC) heralded a much more market-oriented approach, whilst the creation of the Polytechnics and Colleges Funding Council (PCFC) sector of higher education was a radical change which is not likely to be reversed, even following a change of government. The exclusion of local authorities from the governance of public sector higher education (except for a solitary representative), and the dominance of business and other sectional interests, has marked a significant shift in policy since the 1960s when the binary system emerged.

Yet this superficial picture belies a more complex and somewhat contradictory situation. As has been recently pointed out (*Times Higher Education Supplement*, Editorial, 27 July 1990, p. 44) the old binary division between the university and public sectors is rapidly disappearing but only to be replaced by new boundaries between PCFC institutions and local authority provision. Despite the separation of higher from further education it was accepted in the Act that much higher education would continue within local authority colleges even if this was, in the main, at BTEC and professional levels. However, it is now clear that a good deal of degree-level work is being carried on in such institutions, leaving central government and the PCFC in something of a quandary. The PCFC, as the metamorphosed

National Advisory Body for Higher Education (NAB), is still attempting to establish a firm funding policy, and as such appears to have a somewhat ambivalent attitude towards higher education in local authority colleges. While there has been a move to encourage LEA colleges to become 'associate' institutions of polytechnics or colleges of higher education in order that the business of funding – especially competitive funding – can be carried out with relative ease, many of the former have sought to retain their own integrity. In addition, other LEA colleges such as Salford College of Technology have formed close relationships with universities.

These moves to re-establish a stratified (or, sometimes, 'colonial') system of higher education, as a consequence of the more limited role of LEAs prescribed in the 1988 Act, are mirrored by the imposition of market forces on the PCFC and UFC sectors. This is of far greater significance since the ramifications may be such that a number of highly regarded courses, departments and even entire institutions are at risk. This appears to conflict with the appeal to 'excellence' and so it is helpful to cite an example which may serve to illustrate the self-defeating character of the system of competitive bidding for funds. At the end of August 1990 it was stated (Pyke, 1990) that, despite a report the previous week that there was a chronic shortage of physics and chemistry teachers, two institutions were to drop initial training courses in these subjects. The reason for this was clear: institutions, in bidding for funds, were under pressure to back their more popular courses (i.e. non-science) since, if they failed to recruit the student numbers they had promised to PCFC, money would be clawed back, leaving Physics and Chemistry courses to run at a loss. As a result, the conclusion was that it would be better to drop such science courses altogether and concentrate on those which regularly recruit large numbers. This was hardly a recipe for ameliorating a dire situation in which a core subject area of the National Curriculum is at risk.

With regard to the universities, their status is now seen as increasingly subordinate to the wishes of central government, with the Secretary of State for Education together with the Universities Funding Council able to impose their will upon them (Griffith, 1990, p. 98). The extent of this control is illustrated through financial memoranda in which the conditions governing the grant from government to the UFC and from the UFC to the universities are set out. In respect of the latter, university governing bodies are required to designate a 'principal officer' (the vice-chancellor) as the paymaster who will ensure that funds are used in accordance with UFC conditions (Griffith, 1990, p. 99). Yet again, the ideology of the free market is confronted by the reality of political and bureaucratic control.

However, beneath all this, the 1988 Act has bequeathed a situation in which the very survival of higher education institutions is at risk. In other times, this would be cause for great concern among politicians of whichever party. The consensus which greeted the Robbins Report of 1963 and its proposals to expand the university sector, plus a similar response to the 1966 White Paper on the creation of polytechnics, has been shattered by the politics of the 1980s and 1990s. The introduction of the competitive ethos has had the result of encouraging mergers and 'rationalization' of resources throughout the higher education sector. Whilst this has its antecedents in the 1970s when there were a large number of mergers in the public sector, resulting in the formation of new and expanded polytechnics as well as colleges and institutes of higher education, the 1980s saw mergers in the university field. This could particularly be seen amongst the colleges of London University (with, for example, Chelsea merging with King's, and Westfield with Queen Mary colleges).

The 1988 Act, however, brought a new edge to the situation. With the incorporation of the polytechnics and higher education colleges, and with the creation of centralized funding mechanisms for both the university and non-university sectors, competition between the sectors increased sharply. Not surprisingly, the PCFC institutions have been able to make more headway than the universities when confronted with the business of competitive bidding. This has been due somewhat to the establishment by the UFC of a 'price cartel' (*Times Higher Education Supplement*, Editorial, 29 June 1990, p. 44) in which a list of guide prices was published. Although universities were invited to make lower bids, in fact very few did so, resulting in relatively high unit costs, with half the bids turned down by the UFC and a predicted cut of at least 50 per cent in student growth targets (Griffiths, 1990).

The outcome of this would seem to have benefited the polytechnics and colleges, since either university expansion would be halted or unit costs would have to be reduced to the extent that standards might be seen to suffer. If, on top of this, an increasing number of universities curtail their research programmes, the binary divide will be effectively ended, if it has not been so already.

THE FUTURE OF POST-16 EDUCATION AND TRAINING: TOWARDS A UNIFIED POLICY

A central theme of this chapter is that the current confused and incoherent state of post-16 education and training continues largely as a result of the decisions of legislators. Despite the 'strategic' role which has been preserved for LEAs by the Act, it is apparent that,

> the LEAs will be in a much weaker position than the technical instruction committees were in the 1890s, and this situation will ... be further exacerbated by current demographic trends and by other factors such as the emergence of the training and enterprise councils. (Sharp, 1990, p. 119)

On the other hand, if local authorities have had much of their power and influence cut away it does not necessarily mean that their role in post-16 education and training has been ended altogether. A good deal will depend on the strength of their revenue base and the extent to which they are able to resist central government interference, especially in relation to the poll tax. However, there is also the possibility that the generation of new ideas regarding post-compulsory education will provide a counterweight to the narrow perspectives of employer-led vocationalism. Much depends on the timing and cogency of such ideas since, with a change of political direction, they could help put LEAs back into the picture.

Such are the views which have emanated from the Institute for Public Policy Research (IPPR) (Nash, 1990). The suggestion here is for a comprehensive baccalaureate, comprising both vocational and academic dimensions, taken through part-time and full-time modes (or a combination of both). The proposals, published in *A British 'Baccalauréat': Ending the Division between Education and Training*, are that everyone between 16 and 19 years of age would take an Advanced Diploma, covering: the social and human sciences, natural sciences and technology;

arts, language and literature. The major outcome of this British 'bac' would be that everyone would have the opportunity to gain intellectual, practical and work-based skills. A corollary of this is the proposed establishment of a combined Department of Education and Training and a merger between the National Council for Vocational Qualifications and the School Examinations and Assessment Council. In addition there would be a National Training Authority for employer-based education and a Higher and Continuing Education Authority. The IPPR proposals appear to constitute a return to pre-1980s corporatism and much would depend upon the extent to which the 'bac' together with these new bodies are responsive to the articulated needs of both students and employers, as well as to the influence of the academic community.

If 16 to 19 education is to be revolutionized in the interests of an integrated society might not a similar process occur with higher education? Scott (1990) poses the question as to whether the contradictory and incoherent state of higher education prevailing today is an expression of the so-called postmodernist hegemony of the late twentieth century. Arguably, with its beginnings in the Enlightenment of the late eighteenth century and its manifestations in nineteenth-century science, engineering, social science, Marxism, etc., something which might be called modernism has provided the overarching paradigm, among other things, for education policy. More pertinent, perhaps, is the view that positivistic science plus ideas of social and economic planning, together with some vision of a future society, has constituted the consensual basis for political action in Western society. This may have been the case in the many industrializing countries in the late nineteenth and twentieth centuries, other than Britain. In many respects much of modernism seems to have passed Britain by (save for a brief time in the immediate post-war period, especially in architecture and the New Town movement), so perhaps the much cherished time-warp in which the establishment tends to operate has been the major guide for policy and, thus, the resulting pluralism in higher education becomes intelligible in hierarchical terms.

It is doubtful, however, whether the future of post-compulsory education can be effectively discussed solely in relation to modernism/postmodernism. These concepts are too fraught with ambiguity to be helpful and, given that the analysis of modernism/postmodernism is frequently confined to questions of style, there is a tendency to omit crucial political and economic issues. The cynical imposition of market forces on post-compulsory education and training merely underlines the lack of serious intent on the part of central government and suggests a willingness to sacrifice real productive potential upon the altar of capitalist theology. Universities, polytechnics, and colleges of higher and further education must now be re-examined. Old hierarchies have already become irrelevant in the wake of rapidly changing technologies. Who, for example, are judged to be the experts in information technology (IT) – the products of universities or FE colleges? Experience suggests that the skills, knowledge and understanding associated with IT may be gained in a diversity of ways, not least in the process of being involved with its production and use. The proficiency with which even very young children gain expertise in IT challenges conventional wisdom regarding cognitive development.

Critics will argue that any challenge to the stratified character of post-compulsory education and training will prevent the production of 'excellence' and thereby inhibit Britain's renaissance as a supreme economic power. They will point out that unless we encourage and sponsor the potential elite of the country the result will be a dilution of talent and lost opportunities. Nothing could be further from the truth. Demographic considerations, if nothing else, strongly suggest that unless wider access to all areas of post-compulsory education is given to a diversity of social, ethnic, age and gender groups, any kind of sustained economic growth will be impossible. These issues are taken up in the final chapter of this book, but suffice it to say, at this stage, that some hard thinking must be undertaken by central government and by the major political parties. Such thinking is vital, since the current contradictory state of post-compulsory education, underpinned by the ideology of competition, must be regarded as an indictment of a country which has failed to take itself seriously.

POSTSCRIPT

Since this chapter was written, there has been a change of Prime Minister together with attempts to step back from the wilder shores of Thatcherism. John Major has concentrated the collective mind of his government on the impending general election and, in so doing, has tried to upstage the opposition parties in the realm of post-compulsory education policy through the following proposals set out in two White Papers (DES, 1991a, b):

> Funding and controlling further education and sixth-form colleges through new government appointed quangoes, excluding local authorities from any say in the sector.
>
> Giving schools and sixth-form colleges the right to recruit part-time students and encouraging them to provide vocational courses on the same basis as further education.
>
> Two new diplomas overarching vocational and academic qualifications – one awarded for the achievement of GCEs or their vocational equivalent, the other for A-level and its equivalent.
>
> Ending the distinction between universities and polytechnics, and funding them through a single body.
>
> Offering training credits – vouchers to pay for part-time college courses or other training – to all 16- and 17-year-olds leaving full-time education.
>
> Arming the Government with powers to take the careers service away from the local authorities. (Jackson, 1991, p. 4)

An immediate reading of the proposals suggests that while the abandonment of the binary system of higher education is a virtual certainty, the ending of the vocational/academic divide for 16- to 18-year-olds is not. As far as the latter is concerned, there are echoes of 'parity of esteem' after the fashion of the 1944 Act, where although the National Vocational Qualifications (NVQs) and GCSEs/A-levels will result in the award of the same diplomas, there could well be a fine but not too subtle distinction made. In other words, a young person may be asked whether his or her diploma was primarily 'NVQ' or 'A-level', and, unless prevailing attitudes to qualifications are broken down, educational stratification at this level is likely to remain.

REFERENCES

• Bash, L. and Coulby, D. (1989) *The Education Reform Act: Competition and Control*. London: Cassell.

- DES (1991a) *Education and Training for the 21st Century*, vols 1 and 2. London: HMSO.
- DES (1991b) *Higher Education: A New Framework*. London: HMSO.
- Griffith, J. (1990) The Education Reform Act: abolishing the independent status of the universities. *Education and the Law* 2(3).
- Griffiths, S. (1990) UFC to cut student growth targets by at least 50 per cent. *Times Higher Education Supplement*, 24 August.
- Institute of Public Policy Research (1990) *A British 'Baccalauréat': Ending the Division between Education and Training*. London.
- Jackson, M. (1990) Key training may go to awards body. *Times Educational Supplement*, 7 September.
- Jackson, M. (1991) The Great Race begins. *Times Educational Supplement*, 24 May.
- Libby, D. and Hull, R. (1988) The LEA, the college and the community. In *Planning the FE Curriculum*. London: Further Education Unit.
- Maclure, S. (1990) A test of faith for market zealots. *Times Educational Supplement*, 7 September.
- Nash, I. (1990) The 'bac' for a future with no sixth forms. *Times Educational Supplement*, 6 July.
- *NATFHE Journal* 15(2), March/April 1990.
- *NATFHE Journal* 15(3), May/June 1990.
- Prately, B. (1988) Who's driving the curriculum vehicle now? In *Planning the FE Curriculum*. London: Further Education Unit.
- Pyke, N. (1990) Market-based funding closes training courses. *Times Educational Supplement*, 31 August.
- Scott, P. (1990) Pluralism in diversity? *Times Higher Education Supplement*, 31 August.
- Shackleton, J. (1988) The professional role of the lecturer. In *Planning the FE Curriculum*. London: Further Education Unit.
- Sharp, P. (1990) The Education Reform Act 1988: the provisions for further and higher education. *Education and the Law* 2(3).
- *Times Higher Education Supplement*. Editorial, 29 June 1990.
- *Times Higher Education Supplement*. 27 July 1990.
- Utley, A. (1990) Report on House of Commons Public Accounts Committee enquiry into university funding. *Times Higher Education Supplement*, 14 September.

8

The 1988 Education Act and the Future of Education in England and Wales

David Coulby

CONTRADICTIONS WITHIN THE 1988 EDUCATION ACT AND BETWEEN THE ACT AND OTHER ASPECTS OF GOVERNMENT POLICY

This chapter concentrates on the theme of contradiction to offer some conclusions on the extent to which the 1988 Act actually is contradictory in its main terms and the extent to which it contradicts other major aspects of developing government policy. Having briefly summarized the main issues on this theme, it then goes on to look at the ways in which, by contrast, it is in harmony with other major themes in government policy. Finally, it looks beyond the 1988 Act to see what alternative policies are possible for the progress of education in England and Wales.

Chapter 3 pointed to a major consistency within three sections of the Act – those on the assessment arrangements, open enrolment, and the local management of schools (LMS) – which link together to establish a competitive system between schools. Other chapters have pointed to contradictions between the various sections of the Act and between them and other aspects of government policy. Before going on to consider further the Act's links to other aspects of policy, it is worth re-emphasizing the most obvious contradiction within the Act itself, that between centralization and choice. As the necessary prerequisite of competition and as a theme with strong electoral appeal, choice has been one of the watchwords of government popularism (see Chapter 1). The spurious rhetoric of competition depends on parents as consumers having choice between different educational institutions and ideally between a range of types of such institutions. In order for there to be choice the number of the forms of schooling must necessarily proliferate, producing, though only on a highly regionally selective basis, city technology colleges (CTCs) and grant-maintained schools (GMSs) alongside the more traditional local education authority (LEA) and fee-paying schools. In terms of the management of schools, LMS gives heads, governors and parents as governors, choice over how to allocate the school resources: priorities can be established at school level, away from the dictates of the LEA. At higher education level, the notion of choice maintains the unnecessary and misleading binary divide so that students appear to have a choice between specific types of institution and employers similarly appear to be able to choose the type of graduates they need according to whether they come from a polytechnic or a university.

This rhetoric of choice is largely spurious because, as it is necessary to keep emphasizing, the 1988 Act actually places power in the hands of the Secretary of State for Education and Science. It is overwhelmingly a centralizing Act, taking choice away from all other participants in education and giving it to central government. The National Curriculum is the obvious example, spelling out content in laborious detail and establishing an unparalleled testing industry to ensure that teachers teach it and pupils attempt to learn it. The superficial diversification of the forms of schooling only means that a few parents in a few areas of England and Wales have the choice to determine under which financial arrangements teachers shall teach to their children a curriculum entirely determined by the central government. Opting out itself is another centralizing measure. It allows governors and parents to choose to escape from unpopular LEAs; these may include Conservative as well as Labour it should be noted (Deem, 1990), since parsimonious resourcing can be just as unpopular as equal opportunities policies. However, once opted out, the schools are then actually under the financial control of none other than the Secretary of State. Similarly, the newly independent polytechnics and colleges are now actually more firmly under DES (via the Polytechnics and Colleges Funding Council (PCFC)) control without the buffer of LEA involvement and additional funding. Further, the Secretary of State took, though in the event did not use, unprecedented powers to veto the appointment of senior staff to the new London education authorities brought into existence by the abolition of the ILEA. Which schools should be allowed to opt out, who should be allowed to establish a CTC, which public examination syllabuses should be approved, whether schools (following parental complaints) are being sufficiently Christian in their daily acts of worship: all these and many more matters are now at the determination of the Secretary of State. The government's supporters on the far right have correctly complained that the Act, far from giving choices to consumers/parents, actually takes it away from them in many important respects (Chitty, 1989, Chapter 8). Through a substantial distrust of other major participants in the provision of state education, especially LEAs and teachers (Bash and Coulby, 1989, Chapter 1), central government has resorted to placing a large range of important powers not with parents but with itself.

Turning to contradictions between the Act and other aspects of government policy, again many of these have been noted in previous chapters so it is only the main one which needs re-emphasis here. The main contradiction is between the financial implications of the 1988 Education Act and the introduction of the poll tax and, more particularly, poll tax–capping. As the previous chapters have emphasized, the Act is much more likely to increase public spending on education than to reduce it. To this extent it is in conflict with the broader government strategy of reducing expenditure on publicly provided services. This contradiction is most vividly seen with the introduction of poll tax–capping. In harmony with the centralizing theme in government policy noted above, capping actually takes from locally elected authorities any discretion over the amount of resources they are able to raise. For some of them this may well mean that they do not have sufficient resources for education to enable them to implement the terms of the 1988 Act. This could be in terms of the in-service education of teachers (INSET) or materials they are able to make available to schools for the implementation of the National Curriculum. More drastically, by needing to cut the formula funding to schools, this may mean that they are unable to employ sufficient or properly trained and experienced teachers successfully to provide that curriculum. Thus, one piece of government legislation may make impossible the implementation of another.

THE ACT AS AN ASPECT OF A COHERENT PROGRAMME

This book's theme of contradiction and conflict emphasizes one aspect of the implementation of social policy legislation. It should not prevent the examination of those ways in which the 1988 Act is actually more clearly in harmony, albeit only superficially, with other aspects of government policy. An obvious example here is privatization (see Chapter 1). Many major public monopolies have, over the last eleven years, been sold off in large-scale public flotations – British Telecom, British Gas, and the Water Authorities, to name only the largest. Similarly, legislation on the National Health now allows hospital to opt out of area health authority control. In educational terms, this theme of privatization is appealed to with regard to the CTCs and, in particular, the GMS schools, the number of which Margaret Thatcher wished to see dramatically increase. It needs to be emphasized that this harmony between these aspects of government policy exists only at the level of rhetoric. The GMS schools are not being privatized at all when they elect to opt out of LEA control. They are actually shifting into the control of the DES. Far from being privatized, they are being centralized.

When less well publicized themes of social policy are examined, however, the consistency is rather more than superficial. One theme of the Thatcher administrations, and indeed those which preceded them, is the control of youth. Manifestations of this range from attempting to legislate for the control of football hooliganism to the 'social skills' components of YOP and early YTS courses (Bash *et al.*, 1985, Chapter 7); from attempting to depoliticize the National Union of Students to setting up a government inquiry to consider *Discipline in Schools* (DES and Welsh Office, 1989). It is in terms of the compulsory National Curriculum and the central control of public examinations at 16 + that the 1988 Act fits in with this trend. The traditionalist model of the secondary curriculum, now established by statute, contains only safe, familiar subjects; there are no newfangled and potentially seditious subjects such as Peace Studies or Sociology. Furthermore, the subject-centred curriculum implies a transmissionist mode of pedagogy (see the analysis of the terminology of 'delivery' in Chapter 2) in which pupils are busily engaged only in learning that which the NCC and Secretary of State have set down for them. The subject-centred framework makes it exceedingly difficult to include personal exploration, integrated studies, open-ended investigation, community-based action learning or anything else which might engender, in the wayward minds of young people, ideas and actions other than those entirely supportive of social and economic conformity. Compared to the early pronouncements of the MSC (Bash *et al.*, 1985, Chapter 7), the stress on social control is by no means blatant within the Act. But, in terms of conformist knowledge and conformist forms of knowledge acquisition, it is none the less evident. As noted in Chapter 2, this stress on conformity may itself be in dangerous contradiction with the skills in creativity, communication and team-working needed in the workplace of a post-industrial society.

More obviously in line with current government thinking and policy are those ethnocentric strands of both the Act itself and the emerging National Curriculum which it brought into being. This ethnocentrism is manifested at three levels at least; it attacks regionalism within the UK itself; it attacks multiculturalism, and it attacks internationalism. The Conservative governments have had no intention of acknowledging the regional aspirations of the territorial component nations of the UK. The issue of devolution to Scotland and Wales or to the English regions has never appeared on the agenda. The standing of the Conservative Party in Scotland in particular has been eroded to the almost negligible, yet the Westminster legislature still makes the important decisions for this area of the UK which so resolutely refuses to give it electoral support. The examination of the emerging National Curriculum for History in Chapter 2 showed how this Anglocentrism is also to be reflected in the school curriculum.

The government's opposition to multiculturalism is at its harshest, in terms of the effect on disjointed families, in the 1981 Nationality Act. The rigorous restrictions on immigration and the hostility presented to potential immigrants such as those from Hong Kong typified successive Thatcher administrations. The refusal to give appropriate acknowledgement to the multicultural nature of the society in the UK has been at its most visible with regard to statements and policies on education. Mrs Thatcher's attack on multicultural education at the 1987 Conservative Party Conference (Thatcher, 1987), the hounding of Brent's Development Programme for Race Equality and the subsequent modifications to the Section 11 regulations which this ultimately brought about, the continued refusal to award voluntary aided or controlled status to Islamic schools, the refusal appropriately to implement the European Community's directive on mother tongue (heritage language) teaching, the travestied version of the Burnage Report (Macdonald *et al.*, 1989) used in statements by senior educational spokespersons, are just highlights from a record of cultural intolerance which culminates in the 1988 Act. The attack on multiculturalism embodied in the National Curriculum has already been described in Chapter 2. What is important here is that this is consistent with both other government policy on education and with its wider policies on immigration, race and nationality.

In terms of hostility to internationalism, the government's record can be most clearly read with regard to its policy on the European Community (EC). Reluctance to enter the European Monetary System, Mrs Thatcher's famous Bruges speech which forcefully stated her government's inability to envisage the erosion of the British nation state within a larger unit, and the spectacle of British isolation at every European summit meeting, would have been the main points in this policy perspective had the Secretary of State for Trade and Industry Nicholas Ridley not, in the summer of 1990, had to resign after an astonishing sequence of racist remarks to a newspaper editor about the Germans and the French. It even transpired, after Mr Ridley's departure, that then Prime Minister Thatcher had, in all seriousness, held a seminar on the racial characteristics of the Germans. It is again in the emerging History component of the National Curriculum (see Chapter 2) that these elements of government thinking and policy are most clearly visible. By contrast the regulations on modern foreign languages in secondary schools (again discussed in Chapter 2) are likely to privilege the 'white' languages of the EC but only because this option is seen as preferable to giving appropriate status to 'black' languages.

BEYOND THE 1988 EDUCATION ACT

Some of the intentions of the architect of the 1988 Education Act have already been frustrated. The Pharaonic testing edifice which he had planned, for instance, has already been eroded to a more humble form. Other elements, such as the freeing of the polytechnics and the higher education colleges from LEA control, are probably irreversible. The future of much of the rest of the programme probably rests with the decision of the electorate in the next general election in the UK. In this respect to outline an alternative to the 1988 Act might be seen as to pre-empt the election manifestos of those parties in opposition at the time of its passing. There are two major reasons for not wishing to do this. The first concerns that temptation to reaction mentioned in the first chapter. Simply to repeal the 1988 Act is only a recipe for educational utopia for those people who believe that we were in such a blissful state prior to its introduction. The second reason for not issuing a political manifesto at the end of this volume is linked to this: there is a danger in still seeing educational politics in the terms of the 1988 Act, whereas it is precisely these terms which need to be transcended if there are to be any real improvements in the system that exists now or that which existed prior to the Ruskin speech (see Bash and Coulby, 1989, Chapter 1). What follows is certainly political – any writing on social policy legislation must be political if it is to move at all beyond the explanatory. Furthermore, whilst the previous chapters of this book have been passively political by offering a critique of the implementation of social policy, this chapter is more actively political in that it advocates some alternatives to the original policy. However, it is not politically partisan in that the alternatives it recommends are probably not recognizable by any political party in the UK.

The aims of an alternative policy would be quite different, in many respects, to those of the 1988 Act. Two broad aims can be suggested. Firstly, responsiveness to overseas economic competition must certainly be acknowledged, but in the concrete terms of encouraging a far greater proportion of each age-cohort into further and higher education, rather than in the abstract terms of 'standards'. It is by fully developing the skills and creativity of its population that the UK is most likely to succeed in international competition. The notion that overseas economic competition justifies a return to a nineteenth-century model of public education is nonsensical. Furthermore, international competition can only be responded to appropriately if it is within the terms of the actual role of the UK in the world system at the end of the twentieth century: that role is as a moderately strong economy gradually finding its place in the major global economy of the EC, and a multicultural, cosmopolitan society reluctantly abandoning arcane, one-nation belief systems. The aim of the education system would be to help the economy and the society to accommodate themselves successfully to these ostensibly uncomfortable roles. To achieve this would necessitate some change to both the structure and the content of education in England and Wales. Secondly, the aim of generating a much higher participation rate in educational success is commensurate with that of eroding the elitism and ethnocentrism which currently informs so much of school knowledge. If these two aims are acknowledged then the structures and content of education which currently enforce a divide between academic and technical knowledge, between education institutions and the workplace, are the ones in particular need of reform.

An alternative educational strategy would attempt to bridge the academic/vocational divide. A more polytechnic education (Castles and Wustenberg, 1979) would ensure that all children came into contact with a range of workplaces throughout their school years. Collaboration between educational institutions and other workplaces would aim to erode mutual ignorance and prejudice. It is necessary to stress that this would have to be a two-way process. Many of the criticisms of education from industry and commerce (Weinstock, 1976 and similar outbursts from then to the present day) have been marked by a facile ignorance of the processes of education. Developing knowledge in people from industry and commerce about the conditions of state schooling is as vital as bringing teachers and pupils more closely into contact with the workplace. The commitment would need to be reciprocal. People in industry and commerce would need to engage with teachers in the practice of education. This would leave less opportunity for gratuitous or facile criticism in either direction.

In order successfully to implement educational reform it is above all necessary to have a well-educated, well-motivated teaching force – a factor overlooked by Baker when he was Secretary of State. The significant point which no political party is prepared to acknowledge is that this teaching force must also be well paid. In order to recruit the best graduates, and to keep them in what is a profoundly challenging career, appropriate salaries must be offered. There is more here than the economics of the market place, since pay also implies status and the valuation which society places on its teachers. If a graduate teacher, after working five years in an inner city comprehensive school, is paid half the rate of a solicitor or estate agent with the same level of academic awards and the same years of service, or the same rate as a 19-year-old police constable, then a message is being conveyed to all teachers – and to all young people who might be considering becoming teachers – about their value to society. When this message is amplified by Secretaries of State for Education making repeated pronouncements about 'ineffective teachers', and neither Joseph nor Baker had sufficient good sense to refrain from such invective, the status of this nationally important profession is placed in quite unnecessary jeopardy.

The short-term effects of this are teacher shortages in selective subjects and particular geographical areas. The remedy is not to invent a proliferation of new routes into the profession, thereby undermining its newly achieved all-graduate status, nor is it to introduce bursaries or selective additional payments for students or teachers in particular subjects or particular LEAs. It is certainly not to strip teachers of their negotiating rights so that the International Labour Organisation regards their position as one of the most grave violations of workers' rights anywhere in the EC. Pay scales for teachers need to be introduced which are compatible with salaries for equivalently skilled workers elsewhere in the UK economy, which take account of the senior managerial responsibilities of heads, deputies and heads of department and which pay due regard to classroom seniority. The pay system should be a national one but with nationally agreed area weightings for those areas where there are long-term recruitment difficulties. This structure should then be subject to an annual pay review process parallel to that now operating for the civil and armed services and medical doctors (as, indeed, recently advocated by Kenneth Clarke). This process notwithstanding, teachers' negotiation rights should be restored and the establishment of a national teaching council actively encouraged.

The professional autonomy of the teaching profession needs to be paid appropriate respect. This is not to say that teachers should be able to teach what they like or to run schools in whatever manner suits them. Professionalism need not be synonymous with self-interest. The electorate have a right to be consulted over what is taught to children and young people and on how the large public budget on education is spent. But teachers should be free of the time-consuming and morale-sapping deluge of paperwork which, for instance, has accompanied the implementation of the National Curriculum. Such activities, based on a lack of trust in teachers' professional integrity, only takes their time and energy away from planning, teaching, assessment and feedback. Teachers, as professionals, can then choose how to use their time within systems of national and/or local guidelines. Again this aspect of professionalism could be assisted and formalized by the formation of a national teaching council.

Along with appropriate remuneration and professional autonomy, attention will need to be given to the career-long staff development needs of an all-graduate profession. The devolved arrangements which followed from DES Circular 6/86 (DES, 1986) succeeded in giving LEAs and, to a lesser extent schools, priority in determining the ways in which INSET resources should be used. This meant that INSET programmes were appropriately shifted more towards the policies and initiatives of LEAs and schools and away from the interests and career plans of individual teachers (Coulby, 1987). Some balance would need to be restored in this area in the interest of maintaining a highly educated, high-status profession. This might be done through a notion of entitlement, so that a teacher was allowed so many terms' full-time study for so many years full-time, or part-time equivalent, teaching. This entitlement could be linked either to the needs of their school or LEA or to any planned career development or shift. The entitlement would certainly need to include provision for teachers to take career breaks, either to bring up a family or to work in a different profession, and be provided with adequate refresher training to allow them to re-enter teaching at an appropriate level of seniority.

So as not to dodge the issue of resources, a few comments are made about redistribution. The dramatically changed situation in Eastern Europe means that the UK armed forces based at home and in Germany are no longer needed, if ever they were, in such large numbers. Distracting adventures, such as the UK's over-involvement in the Gulf War, in no way counter the possibility for major defence savings. There is the potential for a substantial peace bonus. A good deal of the peace bonus will hopefully go into rebuilding the industrial base and infrastructure in all the regions of the UK. Some of it would thus come to the vital infrastructure of education. Within the education system itself there could be further redistributions through the winding up of CTCs, the assisted places scheme, the testing bureaucracy and locally or centrally funded places in fee-paying schools and through the abolition of the charitable status of such schools.

Whilst the children currently placed within these forms of provision would still need to be educated, this would be within the context of a state system which could achieve the maximum economies of scale. The resources are available to improve state schooling. What is needed is the political will to shift resources to the area which would benefit the vast majority of children and young people rather than to the establishment of exorbitantly costly white elephants, such as CTCs, which can at best benefit only a microscopic minority.

Once the status and remuneration of the teaching profession was clarified, decisions would need to be made about the future of LEAs. This may well be part of a wider review of local and regional government within the UK: a commitment to which, it seems, will be a component of the manifestos of both major parties at the next general election. Whilst a full review may be appropriate, there are at least five educational considerations which would need to be prioritized. Firstly, the LEA system provides both the flexibility to local needs and the responsiveness to an electorate; to replace it with a system which failed to meet both these criteria would, then, be a loss. Secondly, whatever the result of a review, decisions should be clear and the positive roles of all partners in the education system should be clarified in order to avoid the current death-by-a-thousand-cuts syndrome. Thirdly, there should be an explicit link between the mode of local fund-raising and the expenditure necessitated by national social policy legislation which is to be locally delivered; the temptation to demand particular provision from local authorities and then to deprive them of the ability to raise the necessary revenue must be avoided. Fourthly, authorities responsible for the administration of education should be sufficiently large to support the necessary bureaucracy and have sufficient local wealth to sustain an effective education system (this is not the case in some of the new London LEAs, for instance). Fifthly, the contradiction of central government-funded selective initiatives in education (TVEI, CTCs, LEATGS, etc.), within a national context of financial restraint and poll tax–capping, would need to be re-examined to allow local authorities the flexibility to determine their own priorities within a broad framework.

The arguments for and against a National Curriculum have been discussed elsewhere (Bash and Coulby, 1989, Chapter 4). If a National Curriculum is to be retained it needs to be far less prescriptive, both in terms of form and content, than at present. Perhaps the present core curriculum, along with some of the NCC's dimensions and themes (see Chapter 2) would be sufficient. Certainly, if closer and more beneficial relationships between education and the workplace are to be encouraged, the expansion of scientific and technical study in primary school needs to be consolidated and developed further, though within a more integrated approach to the curriculum at this phase (Ritchie, 1990). On the other hand, the two-tier approach to secondary science should be abandoned in favour of a substantial science curriculum for all pupils. Some broad guidelines for the three core subjects would ensure continuity between schools and satisfy the legitimate demands of parents and employers for entitlement skills and knowledge in these three areas. Abandoning the absurd detail of every syllabus for every subject would give back to schools and LEAs that curricular responsiveness to local circumstances and needs so missing in the National Curriculum as well as freeing primary schools from the tyranny of the subject-led curriculum.

It is tempting at this stage, of course, to include in the National Curriculum stable a whole string of the author's own hobby horses. Multicultural education and equal opportunities, along with the linked issue of the integration of pupils perceived to have special needs, would then become central; the place of England within the UK and of the UK within the EC and the world would be major elements; languages would reflect the diversity of the cities of the UK. But the argument above has been that a partisan National Curriculum of whatever type can only last as long as a particular government or as the whims of an individual Secretary of State. A core curriculum needs to be found sufficiently broad and uncontentious in its outline and necessarily restricted in terms of subject areas to command status and commitment beyond the tenure of a particular political party. Within this there might be an appropriate stress on equal opportunities in the widest terms and also on closer connections with, and relevance to, the workplace than are found in the Conservative National Curriculum.

The testing arrangements are already collapsing under their own weight. In so far as they concern the compulsory testing of children prior to 16 on nationally set and marked tests with publicized results, these arrangements should be abandoned as soon as possible. However, parents do wish to know how their children are progressing at school. In many, especially primary, schools the amount of feedback they currently receive is, at best, scant. Teachers should continue to use their own assessment arrangements for diagnostic or formative purposes. They should also find some coherent way of reporting back to parents and pupils on the nature of progress. It could well be that this is best done through some form of cumulative record of achievement (see Chapter 3) with the associated conferencing arrangements. However, once the broadest parameters have been nationally established, LEAs and schools should be free to work out the forms of recording and reporting arrangements which best suit them.

The commitment must be to improve all schools so that the largest part of the 16+ cohort do not leave school believing themselves to be failures and with little prospect of any further high-status education. This improvement would need to occur in primary and secondary schools across the system. There would be no place for divisive attempts to develop superior education for a few children or to set neighbouring schools at each other's throats in a costly struggle for student numbers. The CTCs could be placed under LEA control or simply and rapidly wound up and places found for their pupils in LEA schools. GMS schools could be transferred back to LEA control, though this would need to be done in an entirely non-punitive way. Deprived of the various state subsidies, it is likely that the fee-paying sector would be considerably attenuated. This attenuation would be furthered by the establishment of a high-status teaching force working professionally within national guidelines in well-resourced LEA schools.

The 1988 Act pays little attention to the schooling arrangements of children perceived to have special educational needs. Indeed many of its proposals seem to undermine the (albeit half-hearted) recommendations of the 1981 Education Act towards the integration of these children in mainstream schools (Russell, 1990). Progress towards greater integration had been painfully slow and, by ignoring the whole issue, the 1988 Act effectively set an entirely different agenda away from special education. The progress towards integration needs to be renewed and with enhanced vigour. An appropriately recognized teaching force with considerably enhanced INSET opportunities would obviously help with this as would the generally improved resourcing of educational institutions.

An important factor here may be school discipline. It is those children segregated into the various forms of special provision on the basis of their behaviour who form the majority of children in segregated provision (Coulby and Harper, 1985). They are also the hardest to reintegrate. Furthermore, disruptive activity in schools, especially secondary schools, is one of the main reasons why many pupils, beyond those involved in such activity, fail to derive the maximum benefit from their education. Indeed, it may be that fear about discipline difficulties, no matter how unjustified, is one of the factors deterring people from entering the teaching profession. The enhancement of the profession may itself be a change from which improvements in this area should follow. More than this, however, is probably needed in the interests of both pupils and teachers and this is an area where effective government intervention could provide tangible opportunities for improvement in schools.

The education of the under-5s is another issue neglected in the 1988 Act and indeed the last Education Secretary to make a commitment to universal nursery education for all children whose parents want it was Mrs Thatcher herself when she graced that position. The universal availability of nursery education might do something to counteract the disadvantages with which some children commence compulsory schooling (though see Tizard and Hughes, 1984 as a correction to facile assumptions in this area). It would certainly be a major improvement on some Social Services nursery provision, on the one hand, or on the inclusion of 4-year-olds in reception classes, as happens in some LEAs, on the other.

The introduction of the National Curriculum and its associated assessment arrangements has done little more than to exacerbate the existing difficulties for the 14 to 16 curriculum and for public examinations at 16+. Whilst GCSE had abolished the binary exam system and encouraged more pupils to take public examinations, many still left school with no public examination success. These pupils were seen by themselves, their peers, their families, and their future employers as having effectively failed their schooling. Of both those who succeeded and those who failed at 16+ too many still had had little or no contact with the workplace or understanding of the ways in which their education was and was not relevant to their future employment. The introduction of the National Curriculum based on grammar school subject disciplines and the addition of another tier of assessment arrangements at 16+ simply led to disarray and confusion. GCSE needs more explicit government support than it has had since Sir Keith Joseph was Secretary of State for Education.

GCSE needs to be widened to include more pupils and this process of widening should be seen as one which will not be complete until all 16+ young people are included in this public exam system. In addition, the two-tier GCSE needs to be consolidated into a common examination for all pupils. An expanded range of examination modes and of subjects and interdisciplinary studies should help in this respect. The curriculum for 14- to 16-year-olds needs not to be narrowed back to the 1920s but expanded to take account of the needs of the next century. It needs to take account of rapid technological and economic change. It needs to provide insight into the process of various workplaces and the relevance of education to these for all children not just for those whom the system regards as likely failures. This is an area where the elimination of ignorance and prejudice on the part of employers is essential. A broad spectrum of intellectual and practical competencies needs to be recognized along with the indispensable connections between personal intellectual growth and social and economic usefulness. The hierarchical pattern of 16+ assessment would need to be replaced with more flexible and transferable modular credits. A broad range of credits could then be accumulated, if necessary beyond 16, by a variety of modes (full-time and/or part-time) to allow young people to develop their credentials beyond 16.

The 16 to 19 phase is another area where there is a widely acknowledged need for reform but where the 1988 Act did little more than confuse the issues. The confusions concern both institutional arrangements and curriculum and exams. The current three-tier post-16 system (A-levels, BTEC, Youth Training: see Chapter 7) unnecessarily limits the number of entrants to higher education, contrary to the best interests of either the young people themselves or the national economy. It severely limits the access to higher education for those in the bottom two tiers whilst for those in the top tier it restricts their practical and technical skills and their knowledge about the processes of the workplace. These curriculum and exam arrangements facilitate structures where the top tier only are taught in either sixth forms or sixth-form colleges and the other two tiers in either FE colleges or the other various outposts of the Training and Enterprise Councils (TECs).

Tertiary colleges offer the opportunity for the comprehensivization of the post-16 phase but their implementation without curricular reform could at best lead to some social integration for young people across a stratified system. It may be that what is needed is some extension of the core National Curriculum so that there is a minimum entitlement for all 16- to 19-year-olds. This would include providing some work experience and technical skills for all, including those traditionally destined for higher education. To use chronological age to describe the educational phase is probably misleading at this stage. The entitlement to further education, including a common core, would be something which young people could opt to take up at any time after the compulsory school stage. Whilst the developing NCVQ may well serve to reduce the number of tiers, at least in certification terms, to two, the difficulty of the restricted subject-range of A-levels will also have to be tackled. The 18+ exam will have to take account of a wider range of subjects; it will not be able to afford to ignore expertise in technology, especially information technology; it should appropriately recognize various forms of work experience. The shift should be towards one wide qualification as an entitlement for all at post-16. As at 16+ this needs to be flexible, transferable, and available in part-time and full-time modes. A modular structure would help to break out of the elitist pressure towards early narrow specialization. Successful completion of such a course should carry automatic access to higher education as a right. This automatic access could be deferred for those going straight into employment.

In respect of higher education itself, the terms of the 1988 Act probably need to be carried further. By merging the two funding councils and giving university status to all the large, mature institutions, an unnecessary and misleading hierarchy at this phase could be abolished. Much of the development needed at this phase actually follows the trends set by the PCFC sector. In order to widen participation, it will be necessary to develop many more part-time and mixed-mode degree courses and to expand the links with FE/tertiary colleges in the provision of Access courses.

The unified funding agency would need to establish clear and explicit curricular priorities. This would be easier within a unified sector. There would be nothing then to stop the shift to equal funding for equivalent courses. However, the move towards elite research-only institutions should be discouraged as more, rather than less, research centres will be needed in both educational and economic terms. Whilst various structures and subject combinations for the first degree will continue to proliferate, care will need to be taken, in terms of the resourcing of higher education, that the standard of this award is not lowered below that in the rest of the EC. The vertical integration of further education alongside higher education could be achieved both through institutional arrangements and by modular and credit accumulation arrangements which encourage the recognition of compatibility of units across different awards. A merged higher and further education provision would help to bridge the academic/vocational gulf at this important phase. It would make an increased range of options – practical, theoretical and vocational – available to a much larger component of the age group.

A comprehensive, egalitarian, technically oriented school system staffed by well-trained and appropriately valued professionals should provide the necessary mass access to an expanded egalitarian, technically oriented but culturally informed higher education system. A modernized, economically strong society needs also to be a democratic and tolerant one based on wide access, pluralistic knowledge and full participation.

REFERENCES

• Bash, L. and Coulby, D. (1989) *The Education Reform Act: Competition and Control*. London: Cassell.
• Bash, L., Coulby, D. and Jones, C. (1985) *Urban Schooling: Theory and Practice*. London: Cassell.
• Castles, S. and Wustenberg, W. (1979) *The Education of the Future*. London: Pluto Press.
• Chitty, C. (1989) *Towards a New Education System: The Victory of the New Right?* London: Falmer.
• Coulby, D. (1987) Urban education: the practice and theory of theory and practice. In Bash, L. (ed.) *Comparative Urban Education: Towards an Agenda* (DICE Occasional Paper No. 10). London: University of London Institute of Education.

- Coulby, D. and Harper, T. (1985) *Preventing Classroom Disruption: Policy, Practice and Evaluation in Urban Schools.* London: Croom Helm.
- Deem, R. (1990) Odd one out. *Times Educational Supplement,* 1 June, p. A30.
- DES (1986) *Local Education Authority Training Grants Scheme: Financial Year 1987–88* (Circular 6/86). London: DES.
- DES and Welsh Office (1989) *Discipline in Schools: Report of the Committee of Inquiry chaired by Lord Elton.* London: HMSO.
- Macdonald., I, Kahn, L., John, G. and Bhavnani, R. (1989) *Murder in the Playground: The Report of the Macdonald Inquiry into Racism and Racial Violence in Manchester Schools.* Longsight Press: London.
- Ritchie, R. (1990) Science in the National Curriculum. In Coulby, D. and Ward, S. *The Primary Core National Curriculum: Policy into Practice.* London: Cassell.
- Russell, P. (1990) The Education Reform Act – the implications for special educational needs. In Flude, M. and Hammer, M. (eds) *The Education Reform Act 1988: Its Origins and Implications.* London: Falmer.
- Thatcher, M. (1987) Speech to the Conservative Party Conference.
- Tizard, B. and Hughes, M. (1984) *Young Children Learning: Talking and Thinking at Home and at School.* London: Fontana.
- Weinstock, A. (1976) I blame the teachers. *Times Educational Supplement,* 23 January, p. 2.

Index